Rollercoaster

A Life in
Twenty-Nine Jobs

STEPHEN MILLER

outskirts
press

To Theo, Alex, and Kieran

Table of Contents

Preface:
Meeting Richard Nixon

Midway through the path of life I met Richard Nixon.

It was not in a dark wood and I was not by myself. There were at least a dozen other people present—conservative and neoconservative writers whom Nixon had invited to an informal question and answer session in a spacious suite at the Waldorf-Astoria. The meeting took place late in 1978, when I was 37 years old.

Four years after resigning from the presidency, Nixon wanted to become a public figure again. He had even drafted a plan for doing so, which he called "Wizard." According to Elizabeth Drew, Nixon "decided that the best way to attain his goal of respectability was to emphasize his credentials as a foreign policy expert, a man known to world leaders." The week before I met him he had given a talk at the Oxford Union, where—Drew says— "he was greeted with boos but ended up receiving enthusiastic applause."

I was not surprised that I had been invited. At the time I was a Resident Fellow in Journalism at the American Enterprise Institute, a center/right think tank in Washington. My job title gave me a certain cachet. The *Washington Post* published several op-ed pieces of mine. Magazines asked me to review books or commissioned me to write essays. In 1980 the *London Times Higher Education Supplement* commissioned me to write a piece about Ronald Reagan's rise to power. *Esquire* called me an up-and-coming neoconservative writer.

Walter Goodman, a writer for the *New York Times Magazine,* interviewed me for an article he was writing about Irving Kristol, who was called the godfather of neoconservatism. I was glad to oblige, since Kristol was responsible for my fellowship at AEI. He had also published several articles of mine in the magazine he edited: *The Public Interest.*

Forty years later, I am no longer a neocon for a simple reason: neoconservatism doesn't exist. It was swallowed up by conservatism, which then metamorphosed into the cult of Trump. I dislike labels, but I would probably call myself a centrist Democrat. I said goodbye to the Republican Party when they nominated Trump for president, but I continue to admire the neocon writers whom I came to know in the late 1970s.

To meet Nixon I flew up to New York from suburban Washington D.C., where I lived, but the plane was late and I arrived at the Waldorf-Astoria about 20 minutes after the session began. After being checked by the Secret Service, I entered the suite—finding myself in a long corridor at the end of which was a spacious room where Nixon was holding forth. I tried to be as unobtrusive as possible, tiptoeing towards an empty seat, but when Nixon saw me he stopped talking, rose from his seat, and went over to greet me. Ray Price, his speechwriter and right-hand man, introduced me to him.

How did Price, whom I had never met, know my name? After shaking my hand and mumbling "glad you could make it," Nixon returned to his seat and began talking again.

An ex-President had interrupted his talk to greet me. When I sat down I muttered to myself: "Incredible!"

For two hours Nixon discoursed on foreign policy. After an hour I could only think of one thing: Would there be a coffee break? I hadn't had a cup of coffee since 5:30 AM. But Nixon kept on talking. He seemed very well-informed about many foreign policy questions, but his answers to questions were lengthy and he spoke in a monotonous voice. If only he were witty like Henry Kissinger.

Two hours passed. I was suffering from a raging headache--probably from the lack of coffee.

I perked up when someone asked Nixon a question about Amtrak. Nixon's response was brusque. "I never thought about it," he said. He went on to say that he took little interest in domestic affairs.

The session had started at 9 AM. It was now 11:30 and I had a lunch date with a friend who was a professor at CUNY Graduate School. I had to leave.

Meeting Nixon was one of several high points in my rollercoaster working life. Five years before meeting Nixon I was an unemployed English professor with no job prospects and a wife and a two-year-old child to support. Fifteen years after meeting Nixon I was out of work again. My job at Radio Free Europe/Radio Liberty had been eliminated. I was 54 with no job prospects.

I didn't know anyone my age who was out of work. My friends were successful academics, museum curators, doctors, CPAs, federal bureaucrats. My wife had a job as an analyst with the Foreign Broadcast Information Service, a government agency that analyses media worldwide, so we wouldn't starve.

Would my being unemployed cause tensions in our marriage? I read recently that in Viking culture a woman could sue for divorce if her husband did not support his wife and children. But I was a useful husband. In addition to opening bottles and jars and making sure our car was in working order, I paid the bills and did most of the shopping and cooking.

I didn't feel that I was a failure. I now was busy doing something I liked to do: writing essays—mainly about eighteenth-century British culture. I had been writing since I was a senior in college—first poems, then later essays.

In the next two decades I published four books and several dozen essays. One book, *Conversation: A History of a Declining Art*, was favorably reviewed in the *New York Times*, the *New York Review of*

Books and the *Times Literary Supplement.*

The next book I wrote, *The Peculiar Life of Sundays,* was published by Harvard University Press, but the book did not sell well though it got reasonably good reviews. I could not get a publisher for my next two books. I was going downhill again. Yet six years later I published a book that was well-reviewed and sold reasonably well: *Walking New York: Reflections of American Writers from Walt Whitman to Teju Cole.*

So my writing career, like my working life, was filled with ups and downs. The literary critic Irving Howe, who published two essays of mine in *Dissent,* wrote a book entitled *Steady Work.* I've never had steady work.

This memoir is about the 29 jobs I've had but it is also about several prominent people I've known. In "The Municipal Gallery Revisited" William Butler Yeats describes several persons he knew and admired. My municipal gallery includes a portrait of John McCormick, the biographer of George Santayana and an amateur bullfighter. He was my grad school advisor. It also includes portraits of two leading American intellectuals: Sidney Hook and Irving Kristol. There also are portraits of two distinguished immigrants whom I met while working in Washington: Jan Nowak and Walter Laqueur. Finally, there is a portrait of Brigadier General Robbie Risner. I never met him, but I feel that I knew him because I read so much about him.

The anthropologist Mary Catherine Bateson once said: "Having to pay attention to more than one thing at a time, thinking about relationships, family, children, as well as about work—and not being able to turn it off—means that women have a capacity for complexity that men have not been encouraged to develop." Is the distinction she makes between men and women accurate? My mind has often been a tangle of thoughts about family, friends, and work.

Working is often stressful but work helps us learn about

ourselves—how well we get along with other people, how well we handle stressful situations. Is the fact that I had twenty-nine jobs a sign that I did not work and play well with others? I don't think so.

A job may be stressful, but not having a job is bad for one's psyche as well as one's income. Samuel Johnson said that idleness is debilitating. "He that will diligently labour, in whatever occupation, will deserve the sustenance which he obtains, and the protection which he enjoys; and may lie down every night with the pleasing consciousness of having contributed something to the happiness of life." Yet Johnson, who slaved away on Grub Street for many years, admitted that work could be a grind. "It very seldom happens to man that his business is his pleasure."

The historian Jill Lepore writes: "We're told to love work, and to find meaning in it, as if work were a family, or a religion, or a body of knowledge." Who is this "we"? When I was growing up no one ever told me to love work or find meaning in it. You worked to make a living.

My jobs have been varied—and so have the topics I've written about. I have written about the banality of evil and the difficulty of buying a lightbulb, about the collapse of the Soviet Union and the playgrounds in upper Manhattan. My wife once gave me for my birthday a box of business cards that read

Stephen Miller, Dilettante

Specialist in Ancient and Modern Literature, International Relations, Public Affairs, the Private Sector, and Creative Writing. Commands a Smattering of Various Languages.

Superficial Solutions,
A Division of Charlatans, Inc.

My wife was kidding—at least I hope she was.

When Paul Theroux turned 80 he wrote: "My life has involved enormous upsets and reverses—many changes of address, as well as illness, wealth, and near-bankruptcy. . . ." This chronicle of my twenty-nine jobs talks about upsets and reverses but it is mostly about an offbeat working life in which failures often led to successes. Every job taught me something about myself—about the skills I have and the skills I don't have.

PART ONE:
BEFORE WASHINGTON

CHAPTER 1

Pre-School, Grade School, and High School Jobs

Job #1: Model

Dickens started working in a blacking factory when he was twelve. I started working when I was four or five—not in a blacking factory but in hot and stuffy photographers' studios. I was a child model. My photos appeared in clothing ads for department stores and in ads for dentists and toothpaste. I had a toothy smile. I was cute.

I did not of course choose to do this job. I don't remember much about it except that it was mildly unpleasant. There were the itchy woolen clothes I had to wear, the glaring lights in the photography rooms, the time spent waiting for everything to get set up. I did this for maybe a year and a half. I have no idea how much I was paid.

Why did my parents subject me to this? Maybe they were hard up for money, since my father often lost his job. If I had 29 jobs, he had 40. My mother at that time had a part-time job. When I was eight or nine she started working full-time.

But I have no quarrel with my parents. The critic Michael Gorra, writing about Philip Roth, says: "Everybody has something to blame their parents for. A mother's smothering love; a father's overbearing attempts at discipline." I never got smothering love from my mother, who was not remotely like the proverbial Jewish mother. And my

3

father, who was often away traveling, never disciplined me for anything. In fact, I spent very little time with him. Did I miss having a close relationship with my father? Not at all. It never even crossed my mind. In the West Bronx where I grew up in the late 1940s and early 1950s it was unusual to see fathers playing with their kids.

My father lost many jobs but always got another one. My mother always had a good job. Her last job was secretary to the head of nursing at Columbia Presbyterian Hospital. In the last decade of her life she had Parkinson's Disease and had to go into a nursing home because she fell a lot. Most people fall apart in nursing homes, but my mother, whose mind was fine, flourished. She joined discussion groups; she participated in plays; she chatted with the staff. She was an upbeat extrovert who had many friends.

My father was also an extrovert but he had a paranoid streak in him and could suddenly turn against people. He would get into arguments with bosses, neighbors, even someone driving by. In my 40s I was driving him somewhere when he said to me at a traffic light: "Why is that jerk [in the car next to ours] staring at me?" I replied: "Why are you staring at him?"

I often was exasperated with my father because he would get annoyed about the silliest things. He also could be embarrassing because he liked to tell corny jokes. He was a travelling salesman like Willy Loman in Arthur Miller's *Death of a Salesman* but he was not remotely like Willy Loman. When he lost a job, he got another one. He didn't fall apart. I guess you could call him resilient.

When I first read *Death of a Salesman,* which many critics consider to be one of the greatest American plays, I was puzzled. "What is Willy Loman's problem?" I said to myself. Why was he so upset? Salesmen get fired if they don't make their sales quotas.

My father, like my mother, was the child of Jewish immigrants from Eastern Europe. But he had a tougher childhood than my mother. His father died when he was a teenager. He left school after the eighth grade. He read newspapers but he never read books.

He was not a complicated man. When he came home from

work, he would have a Manhattan straight up. After dinner he usually watched a boxing match, which I often watched with him. I remember several great boxers: Joe Louis, Sugar Ray Robinson, Rocky Marciano. I remember reading a magazine about boxing.

On weekends my father polished his car and played cards with his salesmen friends. He also enjoyed playing the piano at parties. He lacked the discipline to become a good pianist, but he could pick up a tune on the piano if someone hummed it.

In our crowded one-bedroom apartment in the Bronx, we had a concert grand piano that took up one/third of the living room. My parents slept in the living room on a convertible sofa bed. My brother and I slept in the bedroom. I remember lying awake and hearing my father playing the piano and my parents' friends singing while he played.

I can't remember all the things my father sold wholesale to stores. There was Belgian cookware and English bone china; there were ceramic wall decorations and humorous greeting cards. In our apartment boxes of his samples filled the foyer. He occasionally worked in retail—selling men's clothing in stores in Manhattan—but he hated doing that.

If my father had a good month on the road, we would go out to dinner at a Chinese restaurant. He would always order shrimp with lobster sauce. His highest-level job was as the American sales representative for an English dinnerware company: John Holt & Co. There was a write-up about him in a trade journal, with a picture. The company was not a success in the United States, and six months later they shut down their American operation.

My father liked buying and selling so much that he also did it on the side. He would often buy a car, keep it for several months, then sell it. He would do the same thing with pianos. Coming home from school, I sometimes would see men removing a piano from the townhouse in Teaneck, New Jersey. (We moved to Teaneck when I was fourteen.) A few months later he would buy another piano. The neighbors got annoyed so he had to stop.

5

In his mid-sixties my father went into business for himself. He rented a used-car lot in a sketchy neighborhood in Passaic, New Jersey. He bought cars for $200 at an auction and sold them for around $400. His slogan was "Rely on Eli." But his cars were not reliable —not only the ones he sold but the ones he bought for himself. He sold me a Ford Pinto, one of the worst cars ever made, but he didn't know it was a terrible car.

Once a customer came to his lot and took a car out for a test drive. He complained that it was hard to get the car in reverse. "Where are you going?" my father asked. "To California." "Well, just pull out here and make a right. You don't need reverse." I think he was joking but I'm not sure.

Selling used cars in Passaic was dangerous. Once I answered the phone at my parents' house and a man said: "Is Eli there?" I said he wasn't but I could take a message. "Tell the motherfucker that if he doesn't give me my money back I'm going to kill him." My father always dismissed such threats, but he decided to get out of the used-car business when he came to the lot one day and found all the windshields smashed.

Though my father gave up the used-car business, he continued to make deals. He would read the want-ads with a red pen—circling things he might buy. The strangest deal he made was the trailer home he bought in Boynton Beach, Florida. When my brother first visited my parents in Florida, he noticed that there was something odd about the furniture.

"Dad, why is the furniture so low?"

"It came with the trailer," my father replied.

"Yeah, but who would want such low furniture?"

"I bought the trailer from a sky-diving dwarf," my father said. "I got a good deal."

When my mother had to go into a nursing home in Maryland because of Parkinson's Disease, my father stayed in Florida. A few years later, when he was suffering from prostate cancer, he decided to move up to the Washington area, so I went to Florida to help him with the move. He was selling off almost everything he owned. We were down to odds and ends. A woman who had done a lot of favors for him wanted a metal bookcase. My father liked this woman, but he was in his deal-making mode.

"You can have it for five dollars."

"Dad," I said, "give her the damn thing for free."

He relented. He knew he had gone too far in deal-making.

My father was not a great success in life but he enjoyed many things—buying and selling stuff, playing cards, playing the piano. When he was living by himself in Florida he went on a cruise. He sent me a picture taken on the cruise ship. He is playing the piano and people are standing around singing and smiling.

What did I learn from my oddball father? Maybe I learned to be resilient. Don't brood about losing a job. Don't be like Willy Loman.

Job #2: Newspaper Delivery Boy

In old movies that take place in the American heartland you often see boys on bikes throwing newspapers onto porches. My second job was delivering newspapers, but there were no porches and I didn't ride a bike. In the part of the Bronx where I lived, most people lived in apartment houses. I only delivered the Sunday paper, which often was thick, so riding a bike would have been difficult even if I had one. I used a shopping cart—the kind you see mentally ill people wheeling around. The paper I delivered was the Bronx edition of the *New York Post*.

Taking this job was my decision. I wanted to save up money to buy a bicycle and a baseball mitt.

My first route required a lot of walking. It was a twenty-minute walk on Burnside Avenue to pick up the bundle of newspapers for delivery, and then it was another twenty minutes to the Grand Concourse. The elegant art deco apartment houses on this street were a lot fancier than the apartment house on Sedgwick Avenue where I lived. The lobbies in the Grand Concourse apartments were spacious and most buildings had doormen.

I was about to quit the job because of the long walk, but after six weeks I got a route near my street. There was one drawback. I had to deliver the newspaper to a run-down apartment house on a slummy street two blocks from where I lived. It was dirty and reeked of urine and rotting garbage. I had one customer there. When I knocked on the customer's door to get paid for a month's delivery an unshaven bleary-eyed man opened it part-way. A second later a large German shepherd lunged at me. The snarling dog couldn't reach me because the door was open only as far as the chain on the bolt lock extended.

I never knocked on this door again. I would hold my nose and run up the stairs —the apartment was on the third floor—drop the paper, and run down. I absorbed the cost of delivering the paper to this customer.

I learned from this apartment house that there was a darker world than the world where I lived in. I didn't know anything about alcoholism then, but in retrospect I think that my customer was an alcoholic. Maybe there were alcoholics in the apartment house I lived in on Sedgwick Avenue, but the lobby was clean and never smelled.

I didn't make enough money delivering newspapers to buy a bike, but I did buy a baseball mitt—or, rather, a softball mitt. We played softball on a concrete playground that was a ten-minute walk from our apartment house.

Boys have been throwing or kicking or swatting balls since time immemorial. Galen, who wrote more than five hundred years after Aristotle, recommended ball-games. "There is refreshment common to all exercises, but there are special advantages to exercises with a small ball." A ball-game, he says, is "the most efficacious form of physical exercise because all limbs participate in a balanced way."

Softball wasn't the only ball game we played. We also played stoopball, punch ball, and box ball. The most popular game was stoop ball. In New York the steps leading up to the apartment house door are called a stoop. We played with a rubbery pink ball called a spaldeen. It was safe to use this ball because it wouldn't hurt a passerby and it wouldn't break a window.

We also played stick ball and handball against a brick wall at the back of an apartment house. And we played games that didn't use a ball: ringalevio, which was an elaborate form of hide and seek, and a game called Johnny On the Pony. You bent over, putting your hands on a wall, and then kids jumped on your back. The test was: how many kids could jump on you before you collapsed. Everyone got a turn to be the pony.

My Bronx childhood was filled with sports. In the summer we pitched horseshoes in a vacant lot adjacent to our apartment house. I loved the sound of the clang when I threw a ringer. In the winter we crossed the street to go sledding on the grounds of what was then the uptown campus of New York University. (It is now Bronx Community College.) We also took the subway to go ice skating at Wollman Memorial Rink in Central Park. In the summer we occasionally went swimming in a pool across the Harlem River on Fordham Road.

The ball games were for boys only. There were no parents to watch us, coach us, or scream at us. We formed a softball team by ourselves—raising money to buy t-shirts and arranging games with teams from other blocks. The kids we played with were a mixed bunch ethnically: mainly Jewish and Irish with a few kids of Italian descent. No one paid any attention to ethnic differences. On the street and in the field the only thing that counted was athletic skill.

My rich sports life became a diminished thing when we moved to Teaneck, New Jersey. I still played sports, but basketball rather than softball. It would have been difficult to drum up enough kids for a softball game. I also played ping pong regularly in the basement of a friend's house.

What did I learn from all my ball games? I learned that you need to play—need to do things that have nothing to do with your working life. All my life I've played sports. Now I mainly play tennis.

Job # 3: Hotdog Seller

It is a brisk fall afternoon and I am selling hot dogs at a high school football game. Teaneck High School is playing its main rival, Hackensack High School. I can't pay much attention to the game because the customers never stop coming. I'm busy putting hot dogs into rolls.

At first I disliked living in Teaneck. I missed my friends from the Bronx, whom I did not see. The only way I could visit them was by car but we only had one car and my father used it for his road trips, which were frequent. My mother didn't drive.

In Evelyn Waugh's *Scoop* a character says: "Change and decay in all around I see." I didn't see any decay in Teaneck, a town with well-kept houses on tree-lined streets, but I saw a lot of change. Or, rather, my school life in Teaneck was very different from my school life in the Bronx. In the Bronx I went to DeWitt Clinton High School—an all-boys high school with many black students. Teaneck High School was co-ed and had few black students.

To get to DeWitt Clinton I took a bus and a subway. To get to Teaneck High School I walked for a half-hour. Many classmates drove to school with their girlfriends. I felt as if I was living in the world of *The Adventures of Ozzie and Harriet*, one of my favorite tv shows.

I was two years younger than most of my classmates because I had started school early and I had also skipped one grade of junior high school—not uncommon in New York. I was only fourteen when I was a junior at Teaneck High School; most of my classmates were sixteen.

The two-year difference was mainly a sports problem. It was tough to play basketball—or any sport—with boys who were bigger and brawnier than I was. In high school I was only 5' 6" and 150 lbs. When I graduated from college I was 5'11" and 175 lbs.

The age gap burrowed deep into my psyche, so for most of my life I've assumed that I am younger than my friends or colleagues. Now almost all my friends are younger than I am. All the people I play tennis with are younger than I am.

It took a month or so for me to adjust to going to a coed high school in the suburbs, but by the time I was selling hot dogs at football games I was more or less used to my new life. I enjoyed this job. I liked working fast at a relatively easy task. I think I would have been a good short order cook in a diner.

Job #4: Research Assistant, Aeronautical Engineering Lab

It is the summer of 1956 and I am working in an aeronautical engineering lab at New York University. (It is across the street from where I used to live in the Bronx.) My job is an unusual one for a high school student. According to a local newspaper, which wrote a story about me, I spent the summer working on "important scientific research as a full-time salaried research aide." A picture shows me turning the gauge of a machine and recording data. I look like a future Nobel Prize Winner in physics.

My duties, the article says, "included using a simple electronic calculator to compute data from experiments, attaching stress/strain gauges to test equipment, recording experimental results, and developing technical photographs."

The engineers I worked for were doing government-sponsored research on the strength of metals and other materials. "Research engineers at NYU . . . are trying to find out . . . how to prevent buckling of metals under the high temperature encountered in supersonic aircraft flight. This problem is known as the 'thermal barrier.'"

I got such an interesting job because my mother was the secretary for the head of New York University's Department of Aeronautical Engineering. The scientists were looking for a college student but my mother persuaded them to hire me on a trial basis because—according to the newspaper article—I had "straight A's in math and science courses at Teaneck High." I don't think I got straight A's in these subjects, but I know that I did reasonably well in them.

The article says that working with engineers made it likely that I would major in engineering, but I was not sure what I wanted to study in college. I lacked scientific curiosity. I had a chemistry set and a microscope but I rarely used them.

After doing this job for two summers, I realized that I had no interest in being a scientist or engineer.

Lily Tomlin famously said: "When I was growing up I always wanted to be someone. Now I realize I should have been more specific." When I was growing up, I wanted to be a baseball player, which I knew was impossible since I was only slightly above average as an athlete. I had no fall-back plan. I knew that I didn't want to be a doctor, which was what three of my four closest friends wanted to be. After reading *Bleak House* in college I knew I didn't want to be a lawyer. (For those who haven't read Dickens's novel, it is about lives ruined by endless lawsuits.)

In short, I had no goals, no sense of what I wanted to do with my life. And though I was a good student, I was an unintellectual teenager who liked to play sports and watch sports. The biggest event in my Bronx childhood was watching the New York Giants's Bobby Thomson hit a pennant-winning home run against the Brooklyn Dodgers in October 1951, a homer that was called "The Shot Heard 'Round the World." I ran out into Sedgwick Avenue yelling "the Giants won!" I was a rabid Giants fan when most kids in my neighborhood rooted for the New York Yankees. I occasionally went to the Polo Grounds, where the Giants played, and sat in the bleachers. I never went to Yankee Stadium. I lost interest in baseball when I went to college in 1957, so it didn't upset me when the Giants moved to San Francisco in 1958.

I did have one other interest aside from sports. I liked to look at maps. To this day I am surprised when people tell me that they don't know where a certain state or country is. The only areas of the world that I cannot describe are the numerous countries that line the coast of West Africa and the numerous island nations in the Pacific. In the early 1950s the dominant color on maps of Africa was red—a sign that a country was part of the British Empire.

I have only travelled to Europe and Australia, but I like to read travel books. One of the best is Patrick Leigh Fermor's trilogy about his walk from Rotterdam to Istanbul in the mid-1930s. I enjoy hearing about trips to exotic places. A friend of mine made it his life's mission to visit every country in the world. He didn't succeed because he could not get a visa to Saudi Arabia.

In the Washington area where I live there are many immigrants. A few years ago a guy who was doing pest control for our house had an unusual accent so I asked him where he was from: Sierra Leone. He told me that several family members had died in their brutal civil war.

I've always tried to keep in mind that whatever the difficulties of my struggle to make a living, I've had it easy insofar as I've never had to worry about becoming homeless or having enough to eat. And I've never lived in a country ruled by a dictator or mired in a civil war.

Job #5: Day Camp Counsellor

I am on a bus filled with raucous kids—taking them to camp or taking them from camp. I remember the long bus rides, but I remember nothing about the camp, probably because I disliked this job. Many years later I read Samuel Johnson's remark that "nothing is more hopeless than a scheme of merriment." Camps were schemes of merriment—places where adults tried to keep kids happy by making them do silly things, like singing songs or making lanyards.

Yet sometimes I sing to myself a song I learned in camp— "I'm gonna lay down my sword and shield/Down by the riverside, down by the riverside." I also find myself singing Hebrew songs I learned in my three years in Hebrew School. I have no idea why I do this.

I went to overnight camp twice. Once was for two weeks at a camp in upstate New York run by a Jewish organization. At this camp I struggled in vain to learn how to swim. (A few years later I learned on my own.) The second camp, which lasted one week, was near Riverhead, Long Island. Run by the Boys Club of New York, which my father belonged to, it was a camp filled mostly with non-Jewish working-class kids—a rough bunch. I slept on a hard cot and woke up to the sound of a bugle. I remember trying hard to avoid getting into a fight but when a boy continually razzed me I attacked him. A counsellor broke up the fight.

I disliked going to camp and I also disliked the Boy Scouts, which I quit after two months. We went on a hike in 98 degree weather. My tentmate burned his butt by accidentally sitting in a pot of boiling water. We ate horrible food— Dinty Moore beef stew. I quit the Scouts a week later. I realize that the Boy Scouts teach useful skills. My grad school roommate was an Eagle Scout. He built a cabin for himself and his wife in Western Massachusetts. I panic when I see the following three words: "Some assembly required."

Many years later I played tennis with two guys whose lives were shaped by their summers at camp. One, a retired lawyer, started a program called Global Camps Africa for the children of impoverished South Africans. The other—also a lawyer—had a reunion with campmates every year. When he died his widow spread his ashes on the campgrounds of the camp he had attended.

Before we moved to Teaneck, my favorite summer activity was going with four other boys to Castle Hill Beach Club in the East Bronx. We played basketball and handball there and swam. No adult supervision! George Orwell once said that the British ideal was "the liberty . . . to do what you like in your spare time, to choose your own amusements instead of having them chosen for you from above."

At a family gathering a few years ago, a cousin who has a lucrative exterminating business in Connecticut told me that he hated me when he was growing up. "Why?" I asked. "Because my mother always said, 'Why can't you be more like Stephen?'"

Was I a goody-goody kid who sucked up to adults? I don't think so, but I did get along well with grown-ups. And only once do I remember getting into trouble. My parents were away for one night so I invited two friends over and we consumed a bottle of scotch, which made us shriek with laughter. I heard a knock on the door. I opened it and there were two tall policemen. They said that a neighbor reported hearing screams from a woman. The cops searched the house— even the attic.

My most memorable Teaneck experience was a close encounter with death. A friend was driving me home from a dance. He was going too fast on an icy road. Suddenly the car went out of control. We spun around at least once and ended up facing in the opposite direction. It was a miracle that we didn't hit another car or a tree. I never rode with him again. My friend was very intelligent but odd, and I lost touch with him after we went away to college. (I think he went to the University of Rochester.) His father was a physics professor who wrote a widely used college physics textbook. Many years later I learned that my friend had died at the age of 39. The obituary in the *Times* did not give the cause of death.

In sum, when I graduated from Teaneck High School I knew I didn't want to be a scientist or a lawyer or a doctor, but I did not know what I wanted to be. I had few interests. Aside from watching sports and reading maps, I liked to watch Westerns. There was an old song in a cowboy move, "Drifting along with the tumblin' tumbleweeds." That was me in the summer of 1957.

CHAPTER 2

College Jobs

Job # 6: Dishwasher and Waiter

I am scrubbing pots in the kitchen of my fraternity, Sigma Alpha Mu (Sammy for short). This is hard work, but I get my meals free for doing it. I also waited on tables—an easier job. My right arm would have four plates of food on it as I moved from the kitchen to the large dining room where my frat brothers ate dinner. I had this job during my sophomore year.

In *The Freshman* (1990) Marlon Brando, playing a Mafia gangster, looks around the dorm room of a college. "So this is college," he says. "I didn't miss nothing."

Maybe the gangster didn't miss anything, but my four years at Rutgers University changed me in many ways—all for the better. My social and mental world greatly expanded. For the first time I was living away from home and living with people from a wide variety of backgrounds.

In my freshman year my dorm-mates' study habits varied widely. Two engineering students studied all the time—rarely engaging in dorm chitchat. Two liberal arts majors spent most of their time polishing the shoes they wore for the weekly military drill. At all-male Rutgers College everyone was required to take ROTC (Reserve Officers Training Corps) for two years, either Army or Air Force. This meant two classes a week plus marching and drilling in uniform once a week. The two shoe-shining guys did well in ROTC but they dropped out of college.

I was getting A's in Air Force ROTC, so I was invited with six other students to fly on a C-47, a lumbering WWII transport plane. This was my first flight. When we got to the airport, I became nervous because we were taught how to use a parachute. After the aircraft took off, our instructor said that everyone would get a chance to fly the aircraft for five minutes.

"Are you kidding?" I said to myself.

I was summoned to the cockpit. The flight instructor told me to look at the dials and make sure they were aligned to twelve. I turned the wheel slightly and the hands on the dials moved to the left—and kept on moving. They went past twelve.

"Just look out the window," the flight instructor said.

I looked out and the ground looked as if it were coming at the plane—and everything was cockeyed. My heart was racing. "Sir, I think I've had enough." He let me leave the cockpit.

I liked the other freshmen in my dorm though I didn't enjoy spending half the night talking about either sex or God. When boys talked about sex, they usually bragged. When they talked about God, which was rare, they were inarticulate. I saw no point in discussing something that could never be confirmed or disconfirmed. I was an agnostic then. I still am. But I respect believers as long as they don't regard themselves as morally superior to non-believers.

I remember trying to help a dorm-mate who was flunking calculus. I could not explain it to him and he flunked the course. I tried to help another dorm-mate prepare for the final exam in the required history course, which we called Western Civ. He had taken tons of notes—far too many. He had stacks of 3 by 5 cards. He could not tell the forest from the trees, but he passed the exam.

One day I looked out my dorm window and saw four guys doing amazing things with a ball that looked like a basketball—bouncing it off their legs without letting it fall to the ground. They were soccer players from Hungary. The Hungarian Revolution had taken place a year earlier and many Hungarians had fled the country.

I never played soccer. In college I continued to play basketball, but I also took up tennis. I played intramural football—once. I was a halfback and got the ball and ran a few yards when someone tackled me from behind. I had a mild concussion.

In my sophomore year I went out for the lightweight crew team. I assumed that this sport would require mainly effort rather than athletic skill. I was right about that but it required more effort than I expected. We had to run three miles and use rowing machines before we ever got into a skull. The sport was time-consuming. I would get up early in the morning, run to the boat house, and row for a half-hour. By the time I got to my class, I was so exhausted that I often fell asleep. My grades declined dramatically, so I decided to quit after six months.

In high school I enjoyed my science and math courses, but not my English and history courses. In my first year at Rutgers I loved my history and English courses. My Freshman English class was taught by Maurice Charney, a witty young man who would become a leading Shakespeare scholar. But I was not good at analysing works of literature. I remember puzzling over Chekhov's "Gooseberries" and Joyce's "Araby." I decided to major in economics.

In the second semester of my sophomore year I changed my major to English—probably because for the first time I got an A on an English paper. It was in a course on Chaucer. This course changed my life. I became a big reader. The American essayist Logan Pearsall Smith said: "People say that life is the thing, but I prefer reading." I liked reading so much that I quit the college radio station, where I hosted a jazz program.

I never played cards, which was a popular activity for liberal arts majors. My roommate was a pre-med major, so he had no time for cards. I remember that a friend who was a philosophy major wanted me to be the fourth in a game of bridge. I reluctantly agreed to play. After an hour, he said: "You are the worst bridge player I've ever met."

Many years later my tennis buddies would invite me to take part in their weekly poker game, but I always declined.

In my junior year I no longer worked in the fraternity. I gradually stopped going there altogether, and I lost touch with my fraternity brothers.

A few years ago my home phone rang. The name on the Caller ID sounded vaguely familiar so I picked it up.

"Hello, this is _____, your frat brother at Rutgers. Remember me?"

"Yes," I said. But I was not sure that I did. I wondered how he had gotten my phone number.

"So how've you been?" he asked.

I hadn't spoken to him in more than fifty-five years. I laughed. "Are you kidding? How can I answer that?"

"Well, at least you're alive," he replied.

"Yeah."

He was inviting me to a fraternity reunion lunch in Delray Beach, Florida. I said I would love to go but I was not planning a trip to Florida.

Job #7: Copyboy, *New York Times*

"Copy!" a reporter yells. I walk at a fast pace to the reporter's desk in the vast room, pick up the copy, and put it in a pneumatic tube, where it goes to a linotype operator, who produces a galley. It's the summer of 1959 and I'm working as a copy boy for the *New York Times*.

How did I get this great job? Connections. An aunt of mine was a cousin of the *Times's* advertising columnist, Carl Spielvogel. I don't know who talked to whom. All I know is that the *Times* called me for an interview and a week later I was hired. I worked there for two summers.

I rarely talked to reporters, but I had long conversations with the other copy boys, a very bright brunch who went to—or had recently graduated from— Princeton, Columbia, Harvard, and City College. We mostly talked about literature. Several knew a lot about contemporary fiction. They told me to read Saul Bellow, Bernard Malamud, J. D. Salinger, William Faulkner. We also talked about the language bulletins that came from the desk of the assistant managing editor Ted Bernstein, which were illuminating. Bernstein was the author of many books on language.

Many copyboys went on to become well-known journalists for the *Times*. I remember Michael T. Kaufman, an intense and energetic City College graduate who would become a foreign correspondent for the *Times* for many years. When he died in 2010 the *Times's* obituary said, "Mr. Kaufman covered wars, revolutions, politics and America's turbulent 1960s. . . . He traveled widely as a correspondent, interviewing kings, presidents, dictators and the Dalai Lama."

Our boss was Angelo, a short man with thick glasses who also was the bookie for reporters—taking bets on horse races. Angelo never gave us a hard time, but the job required us to be alert and quick on our feet, especially when the deadline for closing the paper was nearing. We went back and forth between the city room on the third floor and the composing room on the fourth floor. Sometimes we had to run errands—picking up packages from other places in the city. After the paper was put to bed we could relax a bit.

The most difficult job was getting sandwiches and coffee for roughly 40 reporters. Inevitably, I would screw up a few orders. "Hey, I said no mayonnaise," a reporter said to me. The reporters were gruff but not nasty.

I often got sandwiches for well-known journalists. I remember Homer Bigart, a famous war reporter who had become the *Times's* leading national reporter. I also remember Herbert Matthews, who gained fame for interviewing Castro a few years before he came to power.

Matthews was widely attacked for insisting that Castro was not a communist. One of Matthews' most famous statements concerning

Castro was made that summer: "The only power worth considering in Cuba is in the hands of the Premier Castro, who is not only not Communist but decidedly anti-Communist."

Forty-five years later I played tennis with a guy who was Matthews's nephew.

"My uncle was very opinionated," he said.

Jobs #8 and 9: Movie Theater Usher; Parking Lot Attendant

I held my flashlight steady as I escorted a young couple to their seats. I was an usher in a movie theater in downtown New Brunswick, New Jersey. In those days some movie theaters had ushers but they were a dying breed. The salary was miserable and there were no tips, but I could see movies for free. I saw two movies three times. I can't remember what they were, but I think one starred Robert Mitchum, one of my favorite actors. I soon asked myself: Why am I spending so many hours by myself in a dark theater? After two weeks, I quit.

I waved my arm, pointing to a space. Being a parking lot attendant at Rutgers University's stadium was in some ways a very satisfying job. I had complete authority. If I waved my hand one way, the car I was directing would have to go that way, though I suppose if it ignored me I couldn't do a damn thing about it. I did this job four weekends in my senior year, when the Rutgers football team played at home. In my senior year I went to see every home game. Rutgers ended the season undefeated. It had a great quarterback, Billy Austin, and an All-American center, Alex Kroll. After I graduated I lost interest in Rutgers football.

Forty-five years later three college friends persuaded me to take a tour of Rutgers University's football facilities. I wasn't interested in doing this but the four of us were spending a long weekend together and I was outvoted. These tours were given to alumni who had donated money to the university. The friend who had arranged the tour—a surgeon—was a donor who followed Rutgers football closely. The four of us met the football coach and we saw the football players' workout room.

After the tour was over, the surgeon said: "Wasn't that great!"

I didn't say anything.

Job #10: Periodicals Clerk: Rutgers University Library

The main job I had during my senior year in college was working as a clerk in the periodicals section of Rutgers University Library. I can't remember exactly what I did, but it involved index cards and keeping track of library subscriptions. The job was easy—giving me plenty of time to read highbrow literary magazines: *Partisan Review, Kenyon Review, Sewanee Review, Hudson Review* and the British monthly, *Encounter.* Many years later I would publish articles in *Partisan Review, Encounter,* and *Sewanee Review.*

Even when I wasn't working I often went to the library. It was an escape from my dorm, where there was always a lot of noise—radios blaring, students yelling at each other. Dorm life was getting on my nerves. A friend who lived on the floor below asked me to wake him up in the morning so that he wouldn't miss class. When I tried to wake him up, he cursed me. When he complained that I didn't wake him up, I told him what happened. He said I should try again, but I refused.

There was also a guy in our dorm who could not take being teased, so he was teased even more. I got teased for going to the library so often and for reading so much, but I didn't care. Once two English majors tried to fool me. "Hey look at this poem," one said. "My friend wrote it. Do you think it's any good?" I didn't know the poem but I knew it was too good to have been written by an undergraduate. "Your friend didn't write this," I said. One guy shrugged: "I bet you didn't know it was by Robert Frost."

In my senior year I took several interesting courses. One was with the highly regarded literary critic R. P. Blackmur, who usually taught at Princeton. Blackmur's lectures were very difficult to follow. I once summoned up the nerve to ask him a question after class. He responded with a cryptic answer that left me even more befuddled.

I also enjoyed a course on Samuel Johnson taught by Paul Fussell, an eighteenth-century scholar who later became known for his books about World War I and World War II. And I enjoyed a course on the English novel taught by Daniel Howard who at the time was married to the novelist Maureen Howard.

Howard urged me to apply for a Woodrow Wilson Fellowship and to apply to grad school in English literature. It had not crossed my mind to do so. Several English majors I knew were planning to go to law school, but I had no interest in doing that. I realized that if I went to grad school in English I would probably become an academic.

My senior year at Rutgers was very rewarding. I won the school's Logic Prize, which was based on a competitive exam. I also won the college literary magazine's first prize for poetry and the Rutgers's English Department prize for essay-writing. I was awarded a four-year fellowship from Cornell in comparative literature and a Woodrow Wilson Fellowship in English, which I could use for Yale. Howard advised me to go to Yale, which was then regarded as the best English Department in the country.

In a personal letter the head of Cornell's Department of Comparative Literature tried to persuade me to go to Cornell. The professor who wrote this letter was Paul de Man, a leading literary theorist who a few years later became Sterling Professor of Humanities at Yale. After de Man died in 1983 the scholarly world learned that he had an unsavory past. As Wikipedia puts it: "A researcher uncovered some two hundred previously unknown articles which de Man had written in his early twenties for Belgian collaborationist newspapers during World War II, some of them implicitly and two explicitly anti-Semitic. These, in combination with revelations about his domestic life and financial history, caused a scandal and provoked a reconsideration of his life and work."

Some colleagues of de Man argued that too much was made of de Man's wartime writings and that de Man, in fact, had helped save the lives of Jews. I don't know if this contention was accurate, but it is clear that De Man hid his past. When reading about him, I often thought of the line from the Beatles's movie, *Help*: "I am not what I seem."

CHAPTER 3

Jobs in My Twenties

Job #11: Driver's Assistant, United Parcel Service

I'm carrying a case of scotch on a long path that has patches of ice on it—delivering it to a house in the posh suburbs of Northern New Jersey. Staring at my feet to make sure I don't step on ice, I hear a dog growling. I look up and see a German shepherd racing down the path—snarling at me as if it is going to attack me. I am about to throw the case of scotch at the dog when suddenly a man standing at the front door of the house yells a command and the dog stops and turns around and slinks back to the house. My heart races for about two minutes.

I am carrying the scotch because I'm working as a driver's assistant for United Parcel Service. It is Christmas break and I'm home from my first semester at Yale graduate school. I had a Woodrow Wilson Fellowship, so why did I take this job? I took it because a friend whose father worked for UPS asked me if I wanted a job that paid well and wouldn't be too hard.

The job did pay well, but it was the hardest job I've ever had—10-hours a day lifting packages out of a truck and delivering them, often up many steps. We started early in the morning and took short breaks for lunch and dinner—finishing each day at around 10 PM. On our meal breaks we sat in diners and silently ate our food. We usually were too tired to talk. When I finished the job I came down with a bad case of the flu and stayed in bed for five days.

In January I returned to Yale with mixed feelings about being in graduate school. I liked most of my classmates but I was getting tired of going to school. My most enjoyable course—on Romantic poetry—was taught by Cleanth Brooks, who was the author of *The Well-Wrought Urn,* at the time considered a classic of poetry criticism. Brooks was a courtly southern gentleman who would never criticize a student. His toughest comment was "Maybe so, maybe so," which meant that you had made a really dumb remark. Twenty years later I ran into him at a conference at the National Humanities Center. "Do you remember me? I was in your class in 1962?" He said he did but I think he was just being polite.

It was not Yale's fault that I was restless. Graduate school was a place for producing professors of English and I was not sure I wanted to be one. I was not able to finish two books that were considered required reading for grad students in English: William Empson's *Seven Types of Ambiguity* and Northrop Frye's *Anatomy of Criticism.* I spent more time in the gym, where I learned to play squash, than in the library.

Garrison Keillor usually begins his Guy Noir spoofs of hard-boiled detective novels with, "It was a dark and rainy night." It was a dark and rainy night when I decided I had enough of graduate school—at least for the time being. I was in my dorm room reading a book by Hannah Arendt (this was not for a class) when I said to myself that I was not going to return in the fall. I needed a break from academia.

Just then there was a knock on my window. I looked up and a guy I knew was sitting on the ledge of my third-floor window, smiling and waving at me. He was a psychology grad student who liked to drink bourbon on the weekends he didn't visit his girlfriend in Boston. I was afraid he might fall, but before I could say anything he moved over to the ledge of the adjacent dorm room. The person who lived in that room was away for the weekend, so I had to find the custodian to get a key for the room and grab the drunken graduate student before he fell off the ledge. Fifteen minutes later the custodian helped me drag the student, who was half asleep, off the ledge and into the room.

At the end of the semester I left New Haven. I thought of Coriolanus's remark to the Romans: "There is a world elsewhere." I would soon find out what this non-academic world was like. Yet since my girlfriend at the time was a grad student in English, I still remained connected to Yale. I often drove up to New Haven on weekends.

But I decided to hedge my bet. Though I left Yale I told the chairman of the English Department that I planned to return after taking a year off.

Jobs #12 & 13: Editorial Trainee, McGraw-Hill; Proofreader: *National Enquirer*

When I was in Yale grad school, I was part of an elite group of future English professors. Now I was just another young man with a college degree looking for a job. I remember answering many ads for jobs in publishing. I landed a job with McGraw-Hill. After finishing a training program, I would become a college textbook salesman. After a week, I quit; I decided that I did not want to be a traveling salesman like my father, even if it meant selling textbooks rather than Belgian cookware.

Two weeks later I got a job as a proofreader for the *National Enquirer*—the sensationalist paper that people glance at while waiting on a supermarket checkout line. The office was a small building in a strip mall—a half-hour drive from my parents' house in Teaneck, where I now was living. I proofread stories about werewolves, Martians, monsters, and murderers. It was an easy job that left time for chatting with my fellow proofreader, who had a Ph.D. in history from the University of Iowa. He was a radical Leftist—the first I had ever met.

After three months I got sick of reading about werewolves and Martians. I applied for a job at the *New York Times* and got one as a clerk in the *Sunday Magazine* section. On my last day at the *Enquirer* I asked my colleague if he was going to continue to work there.

"I dunno," he said, "but I'm not going to work for any bullshit establishment newspaper."

"But the *Enquirer* is bullshit," I said.

"Yeah, but it's obvious bullshit. The *Times* is subtle bullshit."

He thought I was selling out by going to work for the *Times*.

Job #14: Clerk, *New York Times Book Review*

The phone rings and I answer it. A woman asks: "Do you know the name of a recent novel where the main character murders her husband? Someone told me it was really good but I can't remember the title."

During my year as a clerk at the *New York Times Book Review* I got many phone calls along these lines. I wanted to say: "Lady, are you kidding?" Instead I said, "Let me ask around." This was my standard reply to callers who asked absurd questions. I would put the phone down for five minutes, go about my business, then pick it up again. "Sorry, no luck. You might try the New York Public Library."

I began working at the *Book Review* in the fall of 1962 after working one month for the *Sunday Magazine*. At the *Book Review* I had numerous tasks: answering the phone, opening review copies, compiling the bestseller list from bookstore reports, and occasionally writing a headline for a book review.

Am I the only person who has worked for both the *National Enquirer* and the *New York Times?*

This was an easy job and the salary was double what I had been making at the *National Enquirer* plus I could read the books that came in for review. (I had to return them—even those that weren't reviewed—because the *Times* sold review copies.) The *Book Review* staff was friendly and helpful. I remember chatting with Grace Glueck, who would become an art critic for the *Times*.

I became friends with one of the *Book Review* editors—the novelist Charles Simmons. After I left the *Times*, I would have lunch with Charles whenever I was in New York—either at a French restaurant near the *Times* or at the Century Club. Charles was a witty conversationalist—one of the most amusing and charming people I've ever met. He wrote four idiosyncratic novels, including a witty satire of the *Book Review* called *The Belles Lettres Papers*.

Soon after I took the *Times* job, I moved into a small apartment on 112th Street near Broadway. The Upper West Side had not yet been gentrified and my studio apartment, which had one window that faced a courtyard, was in a building filled with prostitutes and alcoholics. I often heard the crash of broken bottles in the courtyard. It was a far cry from the dorm rooms at the Hall of Graduate Studies at Yale.

I spent very little time in the apartment. I went to many chamber music concerts—my passion at the time. A friend of mine knew Walter Carlos, who would soon become famous as the "composer" of *Switched-On Bach*. I never saw him after I left New York but many years later I learned that he became Wendy Carlos. I also read a lot, sitting in diners and luncheonettes, and I wrote a lot of poetry. On weekends I usually went to New Haven to see my girlfriend.

In June I moved into an apartment with a Yale classmate, Morris Dickstein, who would become a well-known literary critic. The other roommate was a graduate student at Yale in German. The apartment, a summer sublet, belonged to the Associate Dean of Columbia University. It was spacious and elegant, but there was one problem: cockroaches. Having grown up in New York, I was used to seeing a few roaches, but this apartment was far more roach-infested than my apartment on 112th Street. When I opened a drawer in the kitchen I saw hundreds of them. The roaches, though, generally stuck to the kitchen, which I avoided. If they came into my bedroom, I killed them.

It was not a happy summer. I was bored with my *Times* job and I was bored with my girlfriend. I got along with my apartment mates, but we had little to do with each other. The grad student in German spent most of his time with his girlfriend, who moved in with him. Morris spent most of his time talking to Marshall Berman, a close friend of his. He came up to the apartment almost every day. Ten years later I would write an essay in which I criticized Berman's book, *The Politics of Authenticity*.

In the fall of 1963 I quit my job at the *Times*, broke up with my girlfriend, and went on a six-week car trip around the United States with a friend who planned to go to medical school in January. We drove 9,000 miles—going to Los Angeles by the southern route, stopping in Miami, New Orleans, and Houston, and driving diagonally through Texas. I remember the locusts swarming in Abilene—covering our car but scattering as soon as we drove off. We returned through the middle of the country—Reno to Salt Lake City to Denver to St. Louis. In Reno there were old ladies working the slot machines; I hate to gamble so I just watched. I remember the endless drive through Kansas. We had to stop every hour to remove the dead insects from the windshield.

If I had stayed at the *Times* would I have been promoted? Robert Hershey, my assistant, became one of the *Times*'s leading economic reporters. I left because I was restless. I was—to quote T. S. Eliot—a "spirit unappeased and peregrine." But maybe that's too highfalutin a description of my state of mind. I went on a trip around the United States because my friend had a cool car—a convertible.

Though we were driving around the United States, my friend and I were not like the characters in Jack Kerouac's *On the Road,* a cult novel admired by beatniks or hippies. I never thought of myself as a beatnik or a hippie. I never felt alienated from bourgeois life. I tried to read Paul Goodman's diatribe, *Growing Up Absurd*: *Problems of Youth in an Organized Society* (1960), which became an important text for the counterculture, but I found it boring.

On my last day at the *Book Review* Nona Balakian, a well-known literary critic and *Book Review* staffer, gave me a book on luck as a going-away present. But luck did not seem to be with me when I got home from my trip. There was a letter waiting for me from the Draft Board. I was required by law to report for a physical in Newark in one week. In all likelihood I would be spending two years in the army.

Job #15: Instructor in English, Fairleigh Dickinson University

I began teaching English at Fairleigh Dickinson University in mid-October 1963—three weeks after passing the Army physical and three weeks before President Kennedy was assassinated. I was grading papers in the dining room of my parents' house, where I was living at the time, when a friend of my brother's came in. "Kennedy's been shot," he said. I ran down to the basement and turned on the television.

The teaching job at Fairleigh Dickinson was an unexpected gift from the gods. Teachers got a draft deferment, so it turned out that I would not be drafted. I did not hate the military, but I did not want to spend two years of my life in the Army. I wasn't worried about getting killed because this was the fall of 1963—before the Vietnam War heated up. Would being in the Army have made me a more disciplined person, a person with goals and objectives? Maybe.

I got the job because an instructor in English had a nervous breakdown. In early October the chairman of the English Department called me: "Could you take over three classes of freshman English right away?" He had my *curriculum vitae* on file because a few months earlier, while working at the *Times*, I had applied for a teaching job.

"I can do it," I told the chairman.

Two days later I was teaching freshman English to night students who had day jobs. Many struggled to stay awake during the two-hour classes.

I told the English Department secretary to notify the Draft Board of my new status right away. Two weeks passed and I still hadn't heard from the Draft Board. I was puzzled, so I drove to the English

31

Department—the university was three blocks from where my parents lived—and asked the secretary if she had sent a letter to the draft board.

"Sorry, I haven't gotten around to it yet. I'll do it this afternoon."

"I need it now," I said politely. "Right now."

I stood there while she typed the letter. I picked it up and drove to the Draft Board office a few miles away in Hackensack.

"You know," the Draft Board secretary said to me, "if you came here three hours later your induction papers would have been in the mail and then it would be almost impossible to change your status."

I didn't know whether to be exhilarated at having such a close call or angry with the English Department secretary. The anger subsided; the exhilaration remained. I would not be drafted!

The chairman of Fairleigh Dickinson's English Department had one request; he wanted me to get an M.A. from Yale. I had been enrolled in the Ph.D. program but Yale was willing to grant me an M.A. provided I passed language exams in French and Latin. A week later I drove up to New Haven. The French exam was easy, but the Latin exam—translating a passage from the *Aeneid*—was hard. My Latin was miserable, but Yale passed me anyway.

When I was in New Haven, I said to myself: Maybe I should return to Yale, since the only thing I'm capable of doing is teaching. In the spring of 1964 I wrote Yale that I would like to return in the fall. I knew that this time there would be no fellowships. Because I was living at home and saving a lot of money, I could probably pay for tuition but I would have to take out a loan or get a part-time job to pay for living expenses.

Once again my plans changed, owing to my "unappeased and peregrine" spirit. A woman acquaintance told me over lunch that she was spending the summer in Southern France. A light bulb lit up in my head: I too would go to Europe for the summer. In June, three weeks after my Fairleigh Dickinson job ended, I took off for Europe. I stayed for three months—spending all the money I had saved. In August, while sitting in a cafe in Vienna, I wrote to Yale that I would not be returning to grad school that fall.

On my flight to Europe—my first commercial flight—I was a bit nervous when we took off. I closed my eyes and was taking deep breaths as the plane ascended when the woman next to me tapped me on my arm. I looked up; she mumbled something and handed me a pamphlet. I looked at the title: *Jesus and the Afterlife*.

I loved wandering around Western Europe, but there were a few unpleasant and embarrassing incidents. On the train to Paris I met a charming English woman and she recommended that I stay at the student hotel where she was staying. When I got there a middle-aged man greeted me effusively, speaking rapid French. He put his arm around me, which made me uncomfortable. Then he followed me back to my room: "Vous faites du sport, n'est-ce pas?" He touched my chest. I backed away. I understood enough French to realize that he planned to bring breakfast to my room. That night I slept in my clothes and was sitting in a chair when he came in the next morning. I told the Englishwoman why I could no longer stay there.

The other incident was about shoes, not sex. I was in Berlin, staying at a student hotel near The Wall. I was running out of money—I mostly ate pea soup at Schnell Imbiss stands—but I had to have my shoes fixed so I took them to a nearby shoe store. Later that day I got a cheap ticket to a Berlin Philharmonic concert for the next day; the guest conductor was Stravinsky! When I went to pick up my shoes the following afternoon, the store was closed. Stores in Germany close on Saturday at noon. So I went to the concert wearing sandals, a worn-out sportcoat, and paints with stains on them. Most men were wearing tuxedos.

In early October I returned to the U.S. on a ship that sailed from Rotterdam. The crossing took eleven days. The ship, which usually served as the University of the Seven Seas, was old and creaky, and the North Atlantic was rough. During the first five days at sea the waves often crashed over the deck. I had trouble brushing my teeth in my tiny cabin because the ship was pitching so violently. I was one of a half-dozen people who showed up for meals. The tablecloths were wet to prevent dishes from sliding. When the weather improved more people showed up for meals. I made several friends whom I swore to stay in touch with after the voyage was over. I never did.

We sailed into New York harbor at dawn on a Sunday morning. When I got off the ship, which docked in Manhattan, I had just enough money to make a phone call to my parents and ask them to pick me up.

Job #16: Reporter, *Bergen Evening Record*

When I returned from Europe, I needed a job. A friend of mine who was working for the *Bergen Evening Record* said I should apply for a job there, which I did, and soon I was working as a reporter for the *Record,* the main newspaper in Northern New Jersey.

I remember my first day on the job. The City Desk editor handed me an accident report. "A teenager died in a car crash," he said. "Get a quote from the family."

"I can't do it," I said. The editor looked at me with disdain. "Ok, you're going to cover these towns." He gave me press releases from five towns in northern Bergen County. For the next four months I went to many meetings: school boards, zoning boards, town councils.

I was glad to have a job but my main concern was avoiding the draft because Vietnam was heating up. Since students usually got a draft deferment, I decided to return to graduate school in January. I knew I could go back to Yale, but I also knew Yale would not give me any money. I applied to Cornell's Department of Comparative Literature and they offered me a fellowship. I also applied to Rutgers's Department of Comparative Literature and they offered me a full scholarship plus a teaching assistantship in the English Department. I chose Rutgers.I would be able to get a Ph.D. without incurring any debt.

Would I have stuck it out as a journalist if the threat of being drafted didn't hang over me? I doubt it. The main problem with being a journalist was my circadian rhythm. I like to get up early and go to bed early. When I was a copy boy at the *Times* I didn't mind staying up late, since it was only a summer job. The *Record* was an afternoon paper so it "closed" much later than the *Times*. I often was in the newsroom typing up my story around midnight.

An editor at the *Record* told me that if I wanted to get ahead in journalism I should write feature stories during my spare time. I didn't tell him that this would probably be my last job as a journalist.

My job with the *Record* was dangerous as well as boring—dangerous because I drove a ten-year-old Ford whose accelerator sometimes stuck to the floor. I would occasionally have to bend down and get it unstuck when I was driving at night.

I should have had the accelerator fixed, but I didn't. A year later, when I was back in graduate school, I sold the car for $25. The guy who bought it said he would pay me in two installments. He gave me $12. I never thought I would see him again but one month later he returned with $13.

In January 1965 I moved into a small apartment in downtown New Brunswick. I was teaching again and I was back in school again. My three-month career as a journalist was over.

Job #17: Teaching Assistant, Rutgers University

Teaching at Rutgers was only a sideline. My main reason for returning to Rutgers was to get a Ph.D. in comparative literature. Now that I was back in grad school again, I knew that my dithering about what to do when I grow up was over: I was going to be an academic, a professor of English or comparative literature.

It felt a bit weird to be the colleague of professors whose classes I had taken four or five years ago, but I rarely ran into them. I spent very little time in my English Department office, which I shared with James Guetti, a full-time professor who had been an All-American football player at Amherst. I liked Guetti, who would write highly regarded works of literary criticism as well as a novel about gambling, but I rarely saw him during my year and half of teaching.

The Rutgers English Department had a strong Amherst presence. Many grad students in English were Amherst graduates. Richard Poirier, the chairman of the English Department, was an Amherst graduate who had taught at Harvard for many years. Poirer was also the co-editor of the *Partisan Review,* which was now based at Rutgers. The other editor was William Phillips, who was one of the founding editors of the magazine.

Since I taught two courses of Freshman English, I had to attend a department meeting about what the reading materials for the course should be. I argued that the course readings should include two or three literary classics since many students would have no other literature class. The majority of my colleagues disagreed. They preferred a course based on materials from popular culture.

Poirier was also interested in popular culture. In "Learning From the Beatles," which appeared in *Partisan Review* in 1967, Poirier argued that the Beatles in particular and popular culture in general should be taken seriously by critics. Poirier's essay was one of many essays that appeared in *Partisan Review* that took a positive view not only of popular culture but also of the counterculture, which was hostile to bourgeois society.

In 1972 Saul Bellow was so unhappy with the direction *Partisan Review* had taken that he wrote a letter to the Century Club opposing William Phillips's membership. Phillips, he said, "intellectually and artistically bankrupted the magazine. Over the last ten years *PR* has become trivial, fashionable, mean, and harmful. Its trendiness is of the most pernicious sort. . . . I think it has become the breeding place of a sort of fashionable extremism, of hysterical, shallow and ignorant academic 'counter-culture.'" I think Bellow exaggerated *Partisan Review's* trendiness, but he did have a point.

During my two and a half years at Rutgers, I met Phillips many times. I took a course in literary criticism with him and I saw him frequently in *Partisan Review's* office because I often went there to pick up my girlfriend, who was in charge of the magazine's subscriptions.

She was also a grad student in comparative literature. Two years later she would become my wife.

Writing in the *Times Literary Supplement* on the occasion of Phillips's death in 2002, Morris Dickstein—my old roommate in the cockroach-infested apartment in Manhattan—said that Poirier "helped make the magazine more sympathetic to new cultural trends." In *Gates of Eden: American Culture in the Sixties* (1977), Dickstein, who was an advisory editor to the magazine for many years, praised Herbert Marcuse, a leading Sixties thinker, calling him a "radical prophet of a new consciousness." Twenty years later Dickstein had second thoughts about Marcuse and other Sixties radicals. "The naiveté of some of the millennial hopes of the Sixties is breathtaking."

Phillips was a man who wanted his day to go smoothly. Once when there was a student demonstration near his office—this was 1968—he complained: "What do they want now?" He defended *PR*'s publication of essays endorsing the counterculture with a typically wishy-washy sentence: "Despite its political mindlessness and anti-intellectualism, some new idealism emerged that you had to be aware of."

One of the essays *Partisan Review* published was "Notes Toward a New Society," written by Marshall Berman, Dickstein's friend. Berman wrote the following countercultural gibberish: "If we want our souls to expand authentically, we must make room for ourselves at the center. In the course of the sixties we have learned to affirm, avidly, militantly, everyone but ourselves. Now we must affirm ourselves as well. We must move, must grow, from apocalypse to dialectic."

I came to dislike the counterculture for its hostility to bourgeois society and its celebration of drug-taking. In my first six months at Rutgers I lived with a grad student in sociology who smoked weed (then called pot) during the week and took LSD on weekends. He did the latter in New York, where his family lived. I tried weed twice and disliked it; I didn't like inhaling smoke. I had no interest in trying LSD. I did not hunger for psychedelic experiences.

"You don't know what you're missing," my roommate said when I told him that I would never take LSD. He handed me fifteen pages of reflections that he had written while on LSD.

"This is incomprehensible," I said after reading three pages.

"You have to be on LSD to appreciate it," he said.

I quarreled with a friend who had been very enjoyable company until he started smoking weed regularly. When he called me uptight for refusing to smoke weed, I got angry.

"I don't give a damn whether or not you think I'm uptight. You just smoke this shit and say stupid things that you think are profound. You are boring!"

End of friendship.

Most grad students at Rutgers were not druggies. Many came from abroad: Sweden, Cuba, Yugoslavia. Miguel Algarin, who founded the Newyorican poetry movement, came from Puerto Rico. I befriended an Egyptian grad student named Abdul Wahab El-Messiri. I called him Habu. After he received his doctorate from Rutgers, he spent most of his life teaching in Riyadh, but he usually looked me up when he returned to the United States for a visit. When I first met Habu he was a cigar-smoking and beer-drinking Marxist. The last time I saw him—a few years before he died—he had become a moderately de-vout Muslim who did not smoke or drink. His wife, though, had not changed. She asked me for a beer.

Habu was an intensely intellectual man who became a leading Egyptian writer on Middle-Eastern politics and literature. We agreed about the counterculture, which he too disliked, but not about any-thing else. I enjoyed his company because he had a good sense of humor and was never self-righteous, but I preferred to discuss litera-ture with him rather than hear him talk about the evils of colonialism, Zionism, and modernity.

Once, when we were having dinner together, he said that he transferred his son and daughter from a public school to a Catholic school in New Brunswick.

"A Catholic school?" I was puzzled.

"Yes," he said. "They have to wear uniforms. I got so sick of the daily arguments between my wife and daughter about what my daughter should wear."

My girlfriend agreed with me about the counterculture, but in the spring of 1965—when we first met—she strongly disagreed with my political views. I had never been interested in politics, but in the early 1960s I began to read Herbert Marcuse, who was widely regarded as the leading thinker of the American Left. Marcuse argued that there was no real difference between the United States and the Soviet Union. In the U.S. the oppression was more dangerous because it was more subtle—a function of capitalist brainwashing, which he called "repressive tolerance." As a result, most Americans suffered from "false consciousness."

My girlfriend was appalled by Marcuse's views. Her parents had fled Hungary in 1948, a few months before the communists consolidated their control over the country. During the Stalinist period her relatives suffered; many were deported to the countryside where they lived under harsh conditions until Stalin's death. Even after Stalin's death their lives were difficult because they were denied advanced schooling and barred from holding certain jobs. Marcuse had refused to support the 1956 Hungarian Uprising. He argued that the revolutionaries were all reactionaries.

In April 1965 I read Marcuse's *One-Dimensional Man: Studies in the Ideology of Advanced Industrial Society* (1964). I concluded that my girlfriend was right about Marcuse. He was an enemy of freedom.

In June 1965 Marcuse spoke at a conference on the future that was sponsored by *Partisan Review.* Sidney Hook, who was the leading American expert on Marxism-Leninism, also spoke. Referring to the Civil Rights Act of 1964, Hook asked Marcuse: "Which would you prefer, a situation in which blacks had no political freedom to vote or one in which they had freedom to vote but chose wrongly?"

Marcuse replied, "I would prefer that they did not have the freedom to vote if they are going to make the wrong use of their freedom."

Marcuse was, in effect, saying: Anyone who disagrees with me suffers from false consciousness and therefore should not be allowed to vote.

Though I disliked Marcuse's remarks, and I also disliked a weird pro-counterculture talk by the literary critic Leslie Fiedler, I enjoyed attending the conference. I and several other grad students had drinks with the German poet/essayist Hans Magnus Enzensberger. I gave the English literary critic Frank Kermode a ride back to his hotel. I thought of asking Kermode what he thought of Marcuse, but I decided not to. Driving my beat-up old Ford, with its unreliable accelerator pedal, required all my attention.

Jobs 18 & 19: Forklift Driver, Factory; Night Watchman, Factory

I'm driving a forklift in a warehouse. Moving pallets from one place to another, I feel as if I'm on an amusement park ride. What was on those pallets? I don't remember because this was only a one-week job that I got from an employment agency.

A few weeks later I landed a job that lasted six months: night watchman in a paint factory—from 11 PM to 6 AM. Every hour I was supposed to walk around the plant and see that all was well. If I didn't do this, who would know, but I did it. The rest of the time I read or slept. It was so quiet—and so spooky. I was not armed, but I did have an alarm system that connected to the police station. What would I have done if I had encountered an intruder? Sound the alarm and run.

I took this job because I quit teaching. I needed more time to study for my orals, write a dissertation, and look for a full-time teaching job. The comparative literature department gave me a small grant that was supplemented by income from the night watchman job. By that time I was married, so there was income from my wife's job doing subscriptions for *Partisan Review*. Our expenses were low. The monthly rent for our one bedroom apartment was $90. We had enough money to take the train occasionally to Manhattan to see the New York City Ballet.

My two and a half years at Rutgers were more interesting than my one year at Yale. I had two superb courses—one on medieval troubadour poetry, another on Dante and Shakespeare. I also took a course on literary criticism with a man who became my thesis advisor: John McCormick.

JOHN McCORMICK

I liked McCormick, who is best known for his biography of George Santayana. We often chatted after class. A year later I chose him to be my dissertation advisor.

When I left Rutgers I lost touch with McCormick but thirty years later I reconnected with him with the help of George Core, the editor of *Sewanee Review*. Core, who had published several essays of mine, was a close friend of McCormick's. When Core learned that I had studied with McCormick, he gave me McCormick's address.

For roughly a decade I corresponded with McCormick, who had moved to York, England, after retiring from teaching. After McCormick died in 2010 I learned that he had designated me to be his literary executor. I was flattered but I had no idea what this entailed. Not much, it turned out. His widow—the poet Mairi MacInnes—gave me letters that McCormick had received from many well-known writers who were his friends, including Saul Bellow, Alfred Kazin, and Elizabeth Hardwick. I sent them to the university libraries that housed their manuscripts.

McCormick may have had more jobs than I had. In his memoir *Seagoing*, he writes about growing up in the Midwest during the Depression. He lived with relatives because his mother had died when he was sixteen months old (in the flu epidemic); his father, who struggled with alcoholism, often traveled in search of a job. At fifteen McCormick left home to work for a man who ran bingo games at state fairs. Sometimes his boss ran out of money and he and other fairgrounds hands had to travel by freight car. During those years he worked in "fairgrounds, mills, factories, restaurants, and hotels."

McCormick calls his memoir *Seagoing* because he had always yearned to go to sea, which he first did when he was a teenager. Working in a restaurant in New Orleans, he met a customer who was first mate on a merchant marine ship. McCormick asked him for a job and the man said he would see what he could do. Soon McCormick became a scullion on a Mexican freighter—and, a month later, a deckhand. It was hard work but he learned a lot about seamanship, which came in handy during World War II, when McCormick spent five years in the Navy.

Having left the merchant marine and gone to college, McCormick qualified to be an officer in the Naval Reserve. He first was an ensign on a PC-class destroyer, which chased German submarines. They were not easy to detect. "In our first all-too successful depth charge attack, we found that we had demolished not a submarine but a whale."

McCormick eventually commanded his own PC destroyer. Many years later, he was annoyed when he read that ships of his class were mostly used as training vessels in calm waters. Not true, he says. He was often in very rough seas and in very dangerous situations. He was not "in the forefront of any grand naval battle," but he experienced "intermittent and intense episodes of naval combat."

War took its toll on the psyches of men who had to live in very close quarters for years—rarely spending time on shore. "We were brutalized by the toiling of arid hours, months, years of the war at sea. . . . In the long periods of convoy duty . . . our ability to exist without frayed nerves from the proximity and predictability of others was tested to the edge of madness." The ship he commanded mainly served in the Pacific, but he remembers rescuing survivors of a torpedoed tanker in the Caribbean. Two men were so badly burned that they asked to be shot. They soon died and were quickly buried at sea.

"The war marked me for life," McCormick writes. He looks back at it with a complex mix of feelings. "We had sailed everywhere but hadn't been anywhere, and there was nothing to show for it but churned sea-water and the morose thanksgiving that Hiroshima and Nagasaki had saved us from the invasion of Japan."

After being dischaged from the Navy at the age of twenty-nine, McCormick got a doctorate from Harvard and spent the rest of his life in academia. He admits that he never felt a "calling" to be a professor of literature. "Other horizons signaled invitingly; I could go back to sea, try to live by writing fiction and free-lance articles, become a newspaperman." He had a family, so he decided that it was too risky financially to give up teaching.

A decade later McCormick could have chosen another profession: *toreo* (bullfighting). Planning to write a book about *toreo*, which he calls an art, not a sport, he thought he should attempt to master this art. He had the opportunity to do so when he was teaching in Mexico City; he spent mornings training to be a matador and afternoons teaching courses in comparative literature. A year later he "performed" as a matador. "I survived, disgracing neither Mario [his teacher] nor myself."

McCormick's bullfighting teacher Mario thought McCormick should "embark on a belated career in *toreo*." McCormick, he said, "might even earn big pesos as 'El Norteamericano' in the plazas along the Texas border." McCormick assured him that "I already had a profession."

McCormick says that his year learning to be a bullfighter gave him "a view of reality that I find precious beyond price. In the face of a charging bull, the matador must *aguantar*—endure, suffer—while maintaining his composure. Daily life may charge, horns tossing, and so one must *aguantar* without panic."

CHAPTER 4

Two Full-Time Jobs

Job #20: Instructor in English: Beaver College

Beaver College—what an embarrassing name for a women's college. In November 2000 ABC News reported that "Beaver College, aiming to shed a source of ridicule and boost enrollment, unveiled today a new school name that's seemingly satire-proof: Arcadia University." In a letter to faculty and students the college president said that the old name "too often elicits ridicule in the form of derogatory remarks pertaining to the rodent, the TV show Leave It to Beaver and the vulgar reference to the female anatomy."

Tell me about it. Almost every time I told a man that I taught at Beaver College—a women's college until 1973—I would get a knowing smile or a snicker. (Women did not respond in this way.) This response got on my nerves, and I would sarcastically say: "Very funny, hah hah hah."

In the fall of 1968 I was happy to be teaching at Beaver College, despite its name, because it was the only teaching job I was offered. It crossed my mind that if I had gotten a doctorate in English from Yale I probably would have had many job offers. Friends of mine who had gotten a Yale doctorate were teaching at Princeton, Queens College, and the University of Illinois.

But I had no regrets. At Rutgers I met my wife. Moreover, Rutgers had been a better intellectual fit for me than Yale. I was now mainly interested in intellectual history, not literature. At Rutgers we had to read the major works of Western philosophy for our oral exam. This reading shaped my thinking for years to come.

Beaver College is located in Glenside, which is north of Philadelphia, but we decided not to live close to the college. We rented a townhouse thirty miles away—in Yardley, a town on the Delaware River in Bucks County. It was only five miles to Trenton, where we took the train to New York, which we often did, mainly to see the New York City Ballet.

I did not hate teaching at Beaver but I didn't especially enjoy it. I lacked educational zeal; I didn't care if a student liked a good story or poem, though it was always gratifying when a student showed some enthusiasm for a literary work. I vaguely remember a few outstanding students. (The actress Anna Deavere Smith was in one of my classes, but I don't remember her.) There were many unpleasant aspects to teaching. I had to tell a few students that they couldn't knit in class; I had to wake up students who had fallen asleep; I had to listen to students complain about their grades. What I disliked most was grading papers, which took up my nights and weekends.

Yet I did not think of choosing another profession. I was certain I would remain an academic for the rest of my life.

I did like being in charge of the campus poetry reading series. I was given this job because I had published a half-dozen poems. I met and chatted with four well-known poets before they began their readings: Anthony Hecht, William Stafford, Adrienne Rich, and W. S. Merwin.

I enjoyed talking to Hecht and Stafford but not to Adrienne Rich. She replied to my attempts at conversation with one word and a grim smile. It was clear to me that she wanted to be left alone before her reading, so I bought her a cup of tea at the student lounge and left.

I couldn't have coffee with W. S. Merwin because he was running late. He was the best reader of the four—and the most charismatic figure. I met him at a nearby train station. He was wearing a leather hat and leather chaps, as if he were a cowboy-poet. After driving him to the campus, I was met by a colleague. The three of us were walking to the main building at the college when Merwin stopped and bowed slightly three times.

"Do you need to use the rest room?" my colleague asked.

Merwin gave her a cryptic smile, pointed to the moon—it was a full moon—and mumbled something. I think I heard him saying "Selene," who is the Greek goddess of the moon. He was bowing to the goddess of the moon.

I also liked teaching a course called Literature East/West, which included Japanese novels and Chinese philosophical texts. I read up on Japanese and Chinese culture, yet it goes without saying that I had a very poor grasp of the complexities of these cultures. A student asked what a tea ceremony in Yasunari Kawabata's *Snow Country* meant. "I haven't a clue," I replied.

I taught this course with a young Irishman in the philosophy department who was an impressive lecturer—talking eloquently about Plato and Aristotle without notes. He reminded me of a lecture given by Isaiah Berlin at Rutgers. Berlin dazzled the audience with his ability to speak fluently for an hour about Machiavelli without notes.

My Irish colleague was one of several faculty members whose company I enjoyed over lunch and an occasional dinner party. There was also a young professor of theater who put us in stitches because he could mimic the most pompous members of the faculty.

One of our lunch companions was an anthropologist who could curse like a sailor. She did her anthropological field work in Fiji, where she fell in love with the British security official responsible for tracking foreigners. (He was now living in Hong Kong because Fiji became independent in 1970.) In my last year at Beaver she divorced her husband, a Philadelphia psychiatrist, and married the Englishman. A year and a half later she wrote to say that she would be back in the United States and could we get together. A few weeks later I opened the door and saw a woman who seemed familiar and unfamiliar.

"Joan?" I said. She smiled and graciously extended her hand. "So good to see you again," she said in a genteel English accent. She dressed like an English woman and to my mind even smiled like an English woman. She was not faking it. She had been transformed by her immersion in British society.

Ruth Fine, who taught art, became a lifelong friend. In addition to teaching at Beaver, she was the curator of the Rosenwald Collection, one of the best collections of prints, illustrated manuscripts, and drawings in the world. When Lessing Rosenwald died in 1979, the collection moved from suburban Philadelphia to the National Gallery—and she went along with it. At the National Gallery she curated many exhibitions, including a blockbuster show of Romare Bearden's art.

Ruth was married to the painter Larry Day, who taught at the Philadelphia College of Art. We became good friends and often had lunch together. Once he said he had to change a lunch date because he had forgotten about the reunion with his army buddies, which he went to every year. I learned that he had been on a troopship headed for Japan when they were attacked by kamikaze pilots. A nearby ship got a direct hit and exploded. A few days later he learned that Japan had surrendered.

Larry, like John McCormick, was relieved that he didn't have to participate in the invasion of Japan. Paul Fussell, my professor at Rutgers, felt the same way. Having fought in the European theater, Fussell was supposed to be shipped to the Pacific in order to participate in the invasion of Japan when he learned about Hiroshima and Nagasaki. In 1981 he wrote an essay, "Thank God for the Atom Bomb."

Beaver's English Department was a mix of genteel old women and odd young men. The oddest was a wooly-minded countercultural guru who talked in buzzwords and often walked around with electronic equipment dangling from his neck. Once he was aggressively poking me in the shoulder and saying a lot of nonsense. I grabbed him and shoved him against the wall: "Will you get off my back!" I was surprised that I did this, since I rarely lose my temper. Thirty years later he wrote a positive review of my book on conversation for an online magazine.

Another member of the English Department did not seem odd and I considered him a friend. But four years later, when I was working at the National Endowment for the Humanities, he wrote to me that I had "stabbed him in the back." His application for an NEH grant had been rejected, and he was convinced that it was my doing. I wrote him back that I was not in the division to which he applied and that I knew absolutely nothing about his grant application. He never replied.

One faculty member, a sociologist, influenced my thinking. His mentor had been Philip Rieff, who now may be best known as the husband of Susan Sontag. I had enjoyed Rieff's *Freud: The Mind of a Moralist.* My colleague told me to read Rieff's *The Triumph of the Threatupetic: The Uses of Faith After Freud.* This book, which criticized the notion of personal liberation, influenced my thinking about the counterculture.

"Publish or perish" say the gods of academe. In the late 1960s I had published a few poems, two essays, and several book reviews. In 1972 and 1973 the magazine *Dissent,* edited by Irving Howe, published two essays of mine that were critical of the counterculture: "Is Hypocrisy What Is Wrong?" and "The Politics of the 'True Self.'" I quoted Rieff in the second essay.

Howe said he had discussed my essays with the well-known literary critic Lionel Trilling, who thought I had been one of his students at Columbia. (I never went to Columbia.) So two leading American literary critics were discussing my essays!

As Diane Keaton says in *Annie Hall*: "La-di-da!"

So I published but a year later I perished—that is, Beaver denied me tenure. I was not surprised. The number of English majors had dramatically declined in the four years I had been teaching there, so the English Department had to slim down. Secondly, I had made no effort to be part of the Beaver College community. I spent very little time at Beaver and I hung out with only a handful of faculty members. At a faculty party a professor said to me: "You know, you haven't invited me to dinner and I'm on the tenure committee." He was smiling but

I was not amused. My wife said to me after we left: "We will never invite him to dinner!" I agreed.

After Beaver denied me tenure, I had a year to look for another job. For eleven months I did not get a job—not even an interview for a job. When August 1973 rolled around I was down to my last paycheck from Beaver. Soon our only income would be the $3500 my wife made from her part-time job with *Partisan Review*.

What to do? I applied for editorial jobs with corporations and I also took the United States Postal Service exam. I liked the idea of delivering mail. Many years later I read that the novelist Bernard Malamud at the height of the Depression also took the postal service exam, but he never worked for the Post Office. In 1940 he took a job with the census bureau in Washington. "All morning I conscientiously checked estimates of drainage ditch statistics, as they appeared in various counties in the United States. Although the work hardly thrilled me, I worked diligently and was promoted after three months." A year later Malamud went to Columbia University to get an M.A. in English literature.

In mid-August, when I was about to sign up for unemployment benefits, Lady Luck smiled on me: I was offered three jobs on the same day. The Post Office offered me a job. I liked the idea of delivering mail, but this job would be sorting mail all night. I would hate working all night. The second job offer was from Mathematica, an economics think tank based in Princeton. I would be an editor—working mainly on writing proposals for government funding.

The third job was really two part-time jobs. A colleague at Beaver College called to tell me that Beaver would be willing to give me a part-time job and that she had found another part-time job for me teaching English at Penn State's campus at Ogontz.

"Give me 24 hours to think about it," I said.

I called her back the next day and told her that I appreciated the effort she made to keep me at Beaver but I decided to take the job at Mathematica. She was surprised and disappointed, but I felt certain that I had made the right decision. I didn't want to hang on to academic life by my fingertips. My wife agreed with me that I should take the Mathematica job.

I did not miss teaching. When I was at Beaver College, I would get migraine headaches about three times a year. After I left teaching I never got another migraine.

Job #21: Writer/Editor, Mathematica

In the fall of 1973 I was once again in "the real world"—a world where people went to work five days a week and had two or three weeks of summer vacation. I hadn't been in the real world since the fall of 1964, when I was a reporter for the *Bergen Evening Record*.

I was for the most part happy about this change. The drive to Princeton, where I worked, was a pleasant 25-minute trip on back roads. My editorial job at Mathematica was not especially interesting but it was better than lecturing to sleepy young women. And when I left work at the end of the day I left it mentally as well as physically. I did not have to grade papers or prepare a lecture. At night I could read or write or play with our two-year-old daughter.

Founded in 1968, Mathematica approached public policy questions by means of econometric analysis. After I left Mathematica it continued to grow and now has eight branches in the U.S. and more than 1400 employees who, according to its website, "work across the country and around the globe, partnering with federal agencies, state and local governments, foundations, universities, professional associations, and businesses."

In the fall of 1973 Mathematica was expanding into the field of education, and my first job was editing a proposal to the Department of Health, Education, and Welfare. (The department was abolished in October 1979, when a separate Department of Education was created.) I don't remember the details of the proposal except that it was loaded with educational and social science jargon. It was not my job to question this language but to make sure the proposal was reasonably clear and grammatically correct.

The proposal was finished on the last day it could be submitted, so I was told to take the train to Washington and hand deliver it. It was my first trip to Washington since my high school bus trip in 1955. I don't remember anything about Washington, since I took a taxi to the Department of Health, Education, and Welfare, delivered the proposal within two hours of the deadline, took a taxi back to Union Station, and a train back to Princeton.

Mathematica's proposal to the Department of Health, Education, and Welfare did not get funded. Three months later the man who hired me was fired. In the next four months I worked on a variety of editorial jobs, but I felt my days at Mathematica were numbered. I applied for corporate editorial jobs without any success—perhaps because my résumé looked too academic. I decided that I had to apply for teaching jobs.

I landed an interview with Cooper Union, which is in Manhattan—in the East Village. Ten minutes into the interview, it was clear to me that the English Department planned to hire someone else. The interviewers paid little or no attention to my answers to their questions. Two glanced at their watches. When the interview ended one professor asked me if I wanted to have lunch. He seemed eccentric—a lonely soul eager to have lunch with anyone. I said I was sorry but I had to catch a train.

A few weeks later I got a letter from Bennington College in Vermont inviting me to be interviewed for a teaching job. If I remember correctly, Alan Cheuse, who was teaching at Bennington, had written to me about the job opening, so I assume that he mentioned my name to the head of the English Department. I had known Cheuse as an undergraduate at Rutgers—he was the editor of the college literary magazine—and also as a grad student in the department of comparative literature.

I drove up to Bennington in a snowstorm—almost sliding off the road to avoid an oncoming truck. I remember a hectic weekend where I met several faculty members and a dozen students. The morning I arrived I was grilled by members of the English Department. It was not going well, I thought. Suddenly a bearded man's face appeared at the door. I think he was the poet-in-residence. He peered at me and said: "What's the meaning of *The Waste Land*?" I thought about this for a few seconds. "I have no idea," I responded. The head was gone.

My last interview was with the president of the college, an earnest woman who was not much older than I was. I was talking about Paul Fussell, perhaps because I had just read his latest book. To lighten things up, I mentioned that Fussell was known at Rutgers to be a wine snob. I jokingly said: "I prefer to drink Gallo." (Gallo's Hearty Burgundy was a popular cheap wine.) I forgot that a few weeks earlier Cesar Chavez had started a strike against Gallo to support higher wages and better working conditions for workers in Gallo's vineyards. The president of Bennington looked disturbed. "Don't you support the strike?" she asked. I said I did support the strike, but the damage was done.

As I drove away from Bennington, I said to myself: "The hell with them. If they offer me a job, I won't take it." They didn't offer me a job.

Two weeks later I got an interview at Ramapo College of New Jersey because a friend of mine who was teaching there recommended me. The interview went well and I was invited back to team teach a class on the modern American novel with the school's writer-in-residence: Roderick Thorp. During the ten-minute break of the two-hour class, I was talking to some students when a young woman interrupted me. "What effect did John Updike's childhood have on his novels?" she asked. I replied: "It's hard to say." And then I turned away from her to continue my conversation with the other students.

My friend said that everything was going well and that I would probably get a job offer very soon. A week later she called to say that the job fell through. What happened? I learned that at the faculty hiring committee meeting a young woman denounced me as a fascist. It must have been the woman who had asked me about Updike. I've always felt grateful to this woman for preventing me from getting a job that I probably would have hated.

That was my last attempt to get a job in academia.

By now I was at a loss about what kind of job to pursue. Maybe I should reapply to the Post Office. Maybe I should get a job in a diner as a short order cook. I didn't consider myself a failure but one could say that I had failed at journalism and failed at teaching. I thought of Melville's remark that "failure is the true test of greatness." What did he mean by that?

While worrying about how to make a living, I continued to write. I finished a comic novel about a city boy who moves to the country. To my surprise a well-known agent liked it and she assured me that she would find a publisher for it. She was wrong; the novel never found a publisher. I also wrote a play about Byron's last days in Missolonghi, when he was fighting for Greek independence. This too went nowhere.

I had some luck with my poetry. D. J. Enright, who co-edited the English magazine *Encounter* for two years in the early 1970s, accepted several poems of mine. At roughly the same time I reviewed a collection of Enright's poetry for the *New York Times Book Review*. Two years later, when he was an editor at Chatto & Windus, Enright asked me to be the lead poet in a collection of three poets. In 1974 *Treble Poets I*, which included twenty-three poems of mine, was published.

I received a favorable review in the *Times Literary Supplement*, but in 1975 the muse of poetry deserted me. So did the muse of fiction-writing and playwriting. I never wrote another poem, another novel, or another play. But I continued to write non-fiction.

One day in the spring of 1974 I was reading an essay by Irving Kristol in the *New York Times Magazine,* and I saw that he was an editor at Basic Books. "Why not look for a job in publishing?" I said to myself. I knew almost nothing about Kristol, but I assumed that he was not a fan of the counterculture, so maybe he would like the two essays of mine that *Dissent* had published. I included them in a letter inquiring about a job at Basic Books. He wrote back that I should come to see him.

When I met Kristol, he said: "Publishing is a tough business that doesn't pay well. I'm on the board of the National Endowment for the Humanities (NEH). Would you be willing to move to Washington?"

"Yes," I said.

Two weeks later I got a call from NEH asking me to come to Washington for a job interview with the Division of Public Programs, which was setting up state councils in the humanities. A month later I was offered a job.

My wife and I joked that we should pray to Saint Irving, who rescued us from poverty. I could divide my life into BK and AK—Before Kristol and After Kristol.

In the fall of 1974 we moved from Yardley, Pennsylvania to Reston, Virginia, a planned community that is seventeen miles from Washington. I would commute to Washington for the next two decades.

PART TWO:
WORKING IN WASHINGTON

CHAPTER 5

Program Officer, National Endowment for the Humanities

(Job #22)

I walk up to the bar in a restaurant in Miles City, Montana. I am about to order a glass of chardonnay when I look around. There are men standing near me who look as if they came out of a Marlboro cigarette ad of thirty years ago: cowboys, ranchers, rugged working-class men. I decide to order a beer.

Why am I in Miles City, which is in the middle of nowhere—nowhere in this case being the vast and underpopulated area of Eastern Montana? I am here because of my job at the National Endowment for the Humanities (NEH). I am the program officer for seven state committees in the humanities, and one of them is the Montana Committee for the Humanities.

What does a "program officer" do? I was not sure when I started the job and I was not sure eleven months later when I was transferred to another job in the same NEH division.

To get to Miles City, I flew into Billings, where I was met by a charming woman who was the executive director of the Montana Committee for the Humanities. We drove 144 miles to Miles City. This was my first trip to Big Sky country. The sun seemed to take forever to set.

In Miles City we had dinner with a man who was a member of the Crow Tribe, which had been given a grant by the Montana Committee for the Humanities. I enjoyed talking to this man, though I learned very little about the grant his tribe got.

At first my new job seemed great: I liked my colleagues and I enjoyed flying around the U.S. at the government's expense. In the mid-1970s flying was easy. There was no security, so you didn't waste time standing in line. On most flights I took the planes were half empty, so I often had a row of seats to myself. I flew at least twice a month to cities all over the country—to Billings, Montana, Oxford, Mississippi, Huntington, West Virginia, Scottsdale, Arizona, Fargo, North Dakota. I also flew to New Orleans, San Antonio, Nashville, Boston, Chicago, and Pittsburgh. Though I spent a lot of time in meeting rooms, I usually managed to find time for some sightseeing.

There was one scary moment. We were about to land in Pittsburgh when the plane suddenly jerked upwards. The pilot said there was a plane taxiing on the runway we were supposed to land on. There were also a few travel glitches. Once I was stuck in a motel in Bismarck, North Dakota, for two days because there was an ice storm and I could not drive to the airport in Fargo. After finishing the novel I brought with me, I read old *Readers's Digests*. There was nothing worth watching on tv.

Ten years earlier, when I had traveled around the U.S. in a convertible with my friend, I met very few people. Now I met many people—professors, businessmen, educational administrators. In San Antonio I had dinner with a rancher who was on the Texas Humanities Committee. In New Orleans I had dinner with a Jesuit priest who was the Executive Director of the Louisiana Committee for the Humanities. This was a regional meeting, so there were several NEH staffers with me. We ate at one of New Orleans's most famous restaurants: Antoine's.

Having great meals and travelling around the country for free—what was there not to like? But after five months the job was getting on my nerves.

I began to feel that my job was meaningless. Let me explain. Every year the state humanities committees had to submit a proposal for funding. In theory I could recommend not funding a particular state humanities committee if I thought it was doing a lousy job, but in practice that was not possible. The state humanities committees knew they would be funded no matter what I said about their programs. A few years later grants to the states became line items in NEH's budget. In other words, the funds were locked in.

At the state committee meetings I attended I was only an observer. Sometimes a committee member asked me a question but most of the time I was ignored. Some committee members were friendly but others resented my presence.

The other problem was boredom. I was sick of hearing discussions about the nature of the humanities and how they could contribute to public policy questions. The committees were required to do programs that focused on public policy. The head of State-Based Programs said: "The focus on genuine public policy issues is crucial. . . . It is what gives the program its moral urgency." The committees resented this restriction, and in 1977 the public policy requirement was dropped. Congress mandated that the state humanities committees could support a variety of programs in the humanities.

After nine months I was disenchanted not only with my job but with the program in general. I was supposed to be a cheerleader for public programs in the humanities but I didn't feel like cheering. I agreed with the columnist Robert Samuelson, who said: "Do we really need the government . . . to promote vacuous ideals such as better public understanding of the humanities?"

Why were there public programs in the humanities? The academics who pushed for a national humanities foundation thought it would be the sister of the National Science Foundation (NSF)—mainly funding research in the humanities just as NSF funded research in the sciences. But Congress saw it differently. In their view NEH was the sister of the National Endowment for the Arts (NEA).

This was the view of Senator Claiborne Pell, the legislator who was instrumental in the founding of NEH and NEA. Senator Pell said that NEH was too attached to the academic world. In 1975 he urged NEH to find "new ways to disseminate the values of the humanities at the state and local levels." He told the *New York Times* that the "Humanities Endowment has not realized its full potential to provide for the enrichment of American life." NEH, Pell argued, was but a "pale shadow" of NEA; the arts had done "a far better job than the humanities in developing diversified, popularly supported, constructive programs at a popular level."

NEH staffers thought the comparison to NEA was unfair because the arts are inevitably more popular than the humanities. Most people would rather go to a play or concert than to a lecture or panel discussion.

Because Pell was insistent that more NEH funds go to non-academic organizations, my boss decided to take me out of state-based programs and put me in the program for national organizations. In practice this meant that I was supposed to persuade labor unions to apply for NEH grants. One day I had lunch with some bigwigs at the AFL-CIO, who listened impassively to what I had to say. They did not commit themselves one way or another.

Another day I took the train up to New York to meet with officials at the Amalgamated Clothing and Textile Workers Union (ACTWU.) I walked into a room and saw a stern-looking woman and two cigar-smoking men. I said I would only take up a few minutes of their time. I explained what I had in mind.

One of the men shook his head: "I don't think so."

I said that I would help them write the proposal. I said it would be certain to be funded. I mentioned Senator Pell's concern about doing more public programs in the humanities.

"We'll think about it," the woman said. She looked at her watch. My time was up.

Returning on the train to Washington, I decided that I hated the idea of begging organizations to apply for grants. My unsuccessful efforts and my lack of enthusiasm for my job became apparent to my boss. A few weeks later his assistant came into my office.

"Steve, I don't think this is working out. You're not a good fit for this program."

"Yeah." I said.

"So we would like you to . . . ."

"Ok, I get it, I'm fired," I said.

The poor guy felt so awkward doing this. He smiled wanly and left the office. I had not asked him how much time I would have to look for another job, but I found one right away. Two weeks later I was appointed Assistant Director for Higher Education Projects in NEH's Division of Education. I had moved upwards—more money—and also moved downwards—from the twelfth floor to the seventh floor.

How did I get this job so quickly? I don't remember the details but probably Irving Kristol was behind it. The new head of the Division of Education, Abraham Ascher, was a historian who had been a colleague of Kristol's wife—the historian Gertrude Himmelfarb—at Brooklyn College. Kristol may have mentioned my name to him.

It may have helped that in the past two years I had published essays in two publications that Kristol had worked for and wrote for: *Commentary* and *Encounter.* In 1976 I published "The Poverty of Socialist Thought" in *Commentary,* in which I argued that the socialism espoused by Irving Howe and other democratic socialists was vague in the extreme. I felt slightly guilty about writing this piece, since Howe had published two essays of mine in *Dissent,* but what I wrote was not a personal attack.

My article stirred up a minor buzz. I was invited to a conference on the future of socialism at Columbia University. I was mentioned by a columnist in *TV Guide,* who called my essay a "devastating analysis"; I got requests for the article from professors in Spain, France, England, and Australia. And my essay was translated into Finnish!

I also wrote three articles for *Encounter,* a London-based monthly journal that published leading Western intellectuals. In 1953 Kristol had been one of its founding editors. Some people claimed to be shocked when it was learned in 1967 that the CIA had indirectly supported the publication, but others said it was money well spent. In the late 1970s *The Observer* wrote that "there is no other journal in the English-speaking world which combines political and cultural material of such consistently high quality."

In "A Nice Place to Visit," which appeared in *Encounter* in October 1975, I criticized Frances Fitzgerald's essay about her recent trip to North Vietnam. Praising its leaders for their pragmatism, and saying that the North Vietnamese are grateful for a "government that provides a system of social security for all" as well as an educational network "that is open to all, including adults," Fitzgerald does not mention the regime's cruel Stalinist policies. The regime's leaders, she says, hope for "peace, democracy, national concord" in the South, which the North Vietnamese government had defeated after the U.S. pulled out and refused to give the South Vietnamese government aid. She adds that the North Vietnamese leaders acknowledged that there would be "a fairly long time period of transition, in which they could do the necessary political work in the cities."

Necessary political work: how could a writer use such a chilling phrase? Did not Fitzgerlad know that "political work" meant executing many people and putting others into re-education camps?

Appalled by her article, I concluded: "It is one thing to bow to Necessity, and to be relieved, moreover, that the ghastly war in Viet Nam is over. It's another thing complacently to obey the weight of this sad time by walking away from the bloody stage reassured that all is for the best. We should remember, though we can do nothing about it, that some people will have to endure the 'necessary political work.'"

SIDNEY HOOK

When I was working at NEH Kristol introduced me to Sidney Hook, a leading New York intellectual for more than a half-century. Hook was also on NEH's Advisory Council. A few weeks later Hook tapped me on the shoulder in a Washington drugstore. "Did you write that article attacking Irving Howe?" he asked. He was referring to "The Poverty of Socialist Thought." I said that I did. "You were not tough enough on him," but then smiling he said: "Very good piece!"

In the same issue of *Encounter* that had my piece on Frances Fitzgerald there was an article praising Hook. "It is vivifying to see this man, now in his seventies, at meetings, always alert, untiring in his demonstration of the logical fallacies of the enthusiastic cliche-mongers half his age, never losing his spontaneity or good cheer." After teaching philosophy at New York University for more than forty years, Hook retired and moved to Palo Alto, where he became a senior research fellow at the Hoover Institution on War, Revolution and Peace at Stanford University.

In the early 1980s Kristol praised Hook for bringing "his extraordinary intellectual powers to bear on particular issues of social or political controversy."

For several decades Hook was the foremost scholar of Marxism-Leninism in the United States as well as the leading exponent of John Dewey's philosophy, but he was more generally known for the strong stand he took against Soviet tyranny and communism in general. He was called a Cold Warrior—a pejorative term for many intellectuals but not a pejorative term for Hook. He called Adolf Berle, a diplomat and advisor to Franklin D. Roosevelt, "a fellow cold warrior." In 1981 Hook wrote that most American intellectuals are "either indifferent to the challenges of the Communist world or hostile to the very conception of such a challenge as a manifestation of cold war sentiment."

By the 1950s most American intellectuals were anti-Soviet but they preferred to see themselves as anti-anti-communist because they thought anti-communists suffered—as President Carter put it in a famous phrase— from "an inordinate fear of communism." The author of a book on the young Sidney Hook says Hook "was gripped by an obsessive anti-communism." Another writer, a professor of philosophy at Vanderbilt, said "Hook adopted a vehement anti-Communism which led him to defend the reactionary political views for which he is now notorious."

63

If some writers attacked Hook for being vehemently anti-Communist, other writers implied that Hook was boring because he always wrote about the evils of communism. In *The Truants* William Barrett, who was an editor of *Partisan Review,* writes that Hook was regarded by the magazine's editors as "a kind of Johnny One-Note, clear and forceful but also monotonous in the one issue he was always pursuing." Irving Howe said Hook had become intellectually rusty. "Within that first-rate mind, there had formed a deposit of sterility, like rust on a beautiful machine."

Howe—not Hook—was sterile insofar as he continued to call himself a socialist without clearly explaining what he meant by socialism.

Hook offered an accurate assessment of communist regimes—far more accurate than the assessments of many academics, who were anti-Stalinist but often praised communist regimes in the Third World. Moreover, Hook was not a Johnny One-Note; he wrote books about a wide variety of subjects: *The Hero in History, Pragmatism and the Tragic Sense of Life,* and *The Quest for Being.*

To call Hook a reactionary makes no sense, since all his life Hook called himself a social democrat. Though Hook recognized that "some form of a free enterprise system is a *sine qua non* for the preservation of political democracy," he rejected the notion that the expansion of government inevitably curtails political freedom, which is the argument Friedrich Hayek makes in *The Road to Serfdom.* In the western democracies, Hook argues, "the increase of government intervention into the economy was accomplished by an *expansion* of civil rights and human rights. . . . Today the welfare state or mixed economy . . . seems to be compatible with a vigorous demoratic political life. It is not an inevitable road to serfdom."

In a letter to *Commentary* written two years before he died in 1989, Hook wrote: "So long as we preserve the political processes of freely given consent, the questions of socialism or capitalism are one of degree, of more or less." Hook always argued that "political freedom is the *sine qua non* of every other form of desirable social freedom."

In the late 1970s Hook wrote to me, praising two articles I had written. Hook often encouraged young writers. A friend of mine who was a fellow at the Hoover Institution told me that Hook urged him to write more. In the early 1980s, when I was a Resident Fellow at the American Enterprise Institute, Hook called me twice to comment on something I had written.

Two years before Hook died in 1989 he published *Out of Step: An Unquiet Life in the Twentieth Century*. In this book he says: "the intensity of the animus generated by political differences among intellectuals during the last half century can hardly be exaggerated."

I wrote to Hook, praising the book. He replied: "I deeply welcome your comments on my Autobiography because you are one of the, unhappily, very few in a position to assess its bearings on an understanding of the political past. . . . Current events have borne out what I said in the past about the Moscow Trials, the purges, the Sovet Cold War against the US." He added that the writers who disliked him in the past for being a Cold Warrior "seem to dislike me as much today for being right about the past."

The critic Hilton Kramer called Hook's autobiography "an indispensable text for our times," yet the book is not without flaws. The main problem is that Hook devotes too many pages to the political disagreements he had with many third-rate intellectuals who are not worthy of his attention. "Who breaks a butterfly upon a wheel?" Alexander Pope said in "Epistle to Dr. Arbuthnot." Hook breaks too many leftist butterflies upon a wheel. Or to put it another way: there are too many intellectual dunces in Hook's book just as there are too many intellectual dunces in Pope's *The Dunciad*, which makes the poem heavy going.

But this is a minor criticism. *Out of Step* is a chronicle not only of Hook's life but of twentieth century political and intellectual history. Hook writes well about his Brooklyn childhood, about his philosophical mentors Morris Cohen and John Dewey, about the year he spent in Germany in the late 1920s, about his friendship with Bertrand Russell, and about his encounters with Bertolt Brecht.

Hook admits that "over the years I suppose I have acquired a reputation as a polemicist. . .. I have never wittingly done gratuitous hurt to anyone." Yet he does not suffer fools gladly. He says that Stephen Spender, a poet who was one of the founding editors of *Encounter,* was "notoriously muddle-headed about political matters."

Some observers who admired Hook's political views argued that Hook was tone deaf about religion—and maybe even hostile to religion. Hilton Kramer says Hook's mind "has long been closed to the whole religious dimension of human affairs." This charge is puzzling, since Hook often wrote about the effect of religious belief on the political realm.

The cultural critic Midge Decter said that Hook "did not really respect, and certainly did not come near to comprehending, religious faith in others. . . . There is every reason to think that he ended as he began: an atheist and an anticlerical of a very old-fashioned kind." Decter's view of Hook is misguided. Hook respected religious faith but he worried about the effect religion sometimes had on the public realm. Hook was not in the camp of Voltaire, Diderot, and d'Holbach, who argued that if religion disappeared the world would be a better place. Hook speaks of "the reality . . . of evil"; he agrees with Morris Cohen that there was "an element of intractability in human beings, a kind of perversity or a will to illusion that would almost ensure the presence of a pyromaniac in any Utopia."

Hook praises William Phillips, the editor of *Partisan Review,* for being "level-headed" and "common-sensical." The same could be said of Hook, yet in *Out of Step* he admits that when he was a teenager he did something very foolish. Though he couldn't swim he dived into a pool with the expectation that the young man who dared him to dive would rescue him, but the young man had a panic attack and did nothing to help Hook, who would have drowned if the assistant coach of the swimming team hadn't rescued him. At the end of his autobiography Hook, who admits he didn't learn how to swim until very late in life, talks about the importance of luck and says "I have been rescued from drowning four times."

Out of Step is a great book by a great man—the most important autobiography written by a New York intellectual. The English critic John Gross said that "it is a fearless book . . . and one that nobody interested in the ideological backgrounds of the 20th century should disregard."

CHAPTER 6

Assistant Director for Higher Education Projects, National Endowment for the Humanities

(Job #23)

Some scholars speak of the "fortunate fall"—*felix culpa*—of Adam and Eve in John Milton's *Paradise Lost*. Though Adam and Eve lose their innocence when they are forced to leave the Garden of Eden, they now are fully human because they have gained a knowledge of good and evil. My "fall" from NEH's Division of Public Programs— i.e. being fired— was fortunate in a less profound way: I soon had a better-paying job at the NEH. I became an Assistant Director in the Division of Education.

My "fall" was fortunate in other ways as well. I got along well with my new boss, who became a lifelong friend, and I no longer had to beg organizations to apply for an NEH grant. Many colleges and universities were eager to get federal funds to revise their courses in the humanities.

To put it bluntly, I had a cushy government job that amounted to a tenured position, since it is almost impossible to fire a government employee. Yet two years later I left NEH voluntarily to take a two-year fellowship at the American Enterprise Institute. My wife supported my decision, which made this risky move easier to do. If the AEI fellowship had not been offered to me, I probably would have stayed at NEH for the rest of my working life.

Though my second NEH job was more agreeable than my first NEH job, it had its downside. I was now for the first time in my life a boss—in charge of roughly 10 persons—and I had to deal with tensions among staff members. One staffer rubbed many people the wrong way—grantees as well as staffers. A grantee called me: "I never want to see that person again!" I was relieved when he accepted a job at another agency.

Another problem was potential grantees who tried to ingratiate themselves with me by flattering me. Talking to Harvard University's Academic Dean, I made a banal remark about a book and he said: "That's very perceptive!" I had many conversations along these lines.

My main reason for disliking my job was simple: I did not see why the federal government should give money to colleges to revise their courses in the humanities. I thought the program I ran was a waste of the taxpayer's money.

Some people on my staff thought I was being overly critical of grant applications. A staffer said to me: "You know, if you don't spend the 3.5 million dollars in your budget, you'll get a bad performance review." I was opposed to funding a proposal from Harvard to redesign its introductory course in Western civilization, but the proposal was approved.

I also thought we were funding too many proposals that centered on local history or social history. In the book about NEH that I wrote six years later—*Excellence and Equity: The National Endowment for the Humanities*—I quote the historian Michael Kammen, who praised the burgeoning interest in state, local and family history, yet added that "this reawakening of popular interest in the past . . . has failed to dissipate the woeful ignorance on the part of most Americans about the basic narrative structure of their national history."

Though I had a negative view of the program I ran, I did not have a negative view of everything NEH funded. I supported grants for publishing the papers of leading Americans. An NEH press release in 2021 notes that "NEH grants have helped preserve and increase access to the essential records of American history, including the papers of George Washington, Thomas Jefferson, Abraham Lincoln, and other presidents, as well as those of significant writers, thinkers, and entrepreneurs such as Willa Cather, Ernest Hemingway, Martin Luther King Jr., and Thomas Edison."

I also thought it was a good idea to give grants for preserving deteriorating newspapers and magazines. In my book on NEH I wrote: "We can say with certainty that many scholars in the humanities. . . would find it difficult to pursue their work if the NEH-supported New York Public Library, which spent 1.2 million on book conservation in 1981, were to lose a significant proportion of its holdings through deterioration."

I agree with what Irving Kristol says about the NEH. In 1980 he wrote that "a lot of the money is now simply wasted . . . on all sorts of dubious community and cultural activities. . ..It's now in the business of . . . spreading the money around state by state. ....It has been quite politicized. It still does some good—I'd say half of what it does is perfectly good."

After writing my book on NEH in 1983-1984, I lost interest in the agency. But I recently looked to see if the job I had still exists. NEH has a program that sounds similar to Higher Education Projects. It is called Humanities Initiatives. "Humanities Initiatives at Colleges and Universities strengthen the teaching and study of the humanities at institutions of higher education by developing new humanities programs, resources (including those in digital format), or courses, or by enhancing existing ones."

In two respects this program is different from the one I directed. First, grants have a budget ceiling of $150,000, which is much lower than the budget ceiling for grants when I was at NEH. Secondly, there are now five different categories of grants: Humanities Initiatives at Colleges and Universities; Humanities Initiatives at Historically Black Colleges and Universities; Humanities Initiatives at Hispanic-Serving

Institutions; Humanities Initiatives at Community Colleges; and Humanities Initiatives at Tribal Colleges and Universities. An "Hispanic-serving institution" is an institution of higher education whose undergraduate enrollment is 25 percent Hispanic.

The proliferation of grant categories is an attempt on NEH's part to please Congress by showing that there is a "fair" distribution of grants and that NEH funds do not go mainly to elite academic institutions.

Has NEH's grants to colleges and universities improved the teaching of the humanities? It is impossible to answer this question, but in the past 15 years the number of students who major in the humanities has dramatically declined. In July 2018 the *Chronicle of Higher Education* headlined an article: "The Humanities As We Know Them Are Doomed. Now What?"

In February 2021 the *Chronicle* ran another gloomy article about the state of the humanities in colleges and universities. In "Social Justice, Austerity, and the Humanities Death Spiral," the author argues that "two convergent trends . . . will continue to shape the future of the humanities and social sciences. The first is an increasing emphasis on social justice as the raison d'être of scholarship and teaching. The second is a further ratcheting up of austerity in an area of higher ed that has been decimated by budget cuts ever since the 2008 recession."

Is the decline of the humanities in academia a major problem? The critic Adam Kirsch does not think so. "When the university comes to be seen as the sole custodian of the humanities, both the humanities and the university suffer."

IRVING KRISTOL

While working at NEH I continued to write essays—now mainly for magazines run by neoconservatives, including *Commentary*, the *American Spectator*, and *The Public Interest*. Kristol commissioned me to write an essay on the Washington novel for *The Public Interest*.

Kristol was called the godfather of neoconservatism, but he was also my godfather or—rather—my patron. Without his support I might have ended up sorting mail in the Post Office. He not only recommended me for two jobs, he wrote an introduction to my first book, *Special Interest Groups in American Politics.*

I am indebted to Kristol, but so are many other men and women. Kristol was a one-person employment agency. He helped young men and women get jobs in the government, journalism, academia, and the foundation world.

In 1995 Kristol wrote: "In the past three decades, Washington has witnessed a surge of intellectual vitality." Kristol played a major role in this surge; he helped turn the American Enterprise Institute into an influential think tank. As a result of the magazines he founded—*The Public Interest* and *The National Interest*—neoconservatism became an influential current in the Republican Party.

I could also call Kristol my agent because he recommended me to several magazine editors. In June 1978, soon after I had accepted the fellowship at AEI, he wrote to me: "I am certainly delighted to learn that you will be spending the next year at AEI, writing, writing writing." He said I should write for the *Washington Post* and he would be glad to introduce me to Meg Greenfield, who ran their editorial page. I never did meet Greenfield, perhaps because I was not especially interested in writing op-ed pieces, though in the late 1970s and early 1980s I published several in the *Post.*

Kristol also wrote: "I have had you in mind for some other things in New York, but there is nothing definite at the moment. Perhaps one of these days I'll be in a position to disrupt your life again."

The last sentence gives some idea of Kristol's temperament. There was a playful quality about him. Or, to put it another way, he was always serious but never earnest. He entitled one of his essays: "Confessions of a True, Self-Confessed—Perhaps the Only—'Neoconservative.'"

Kristol was always ruminating about how to increase the likelihood that the United States would be prosperous and politically stable. He never engaged in personal attacks, and—so far as I know—he never responded to personal attacks.

Kristol called himself a "cheerful conservative." I think genial might be a better word because his essays are not always cheerful. He had a dark view of human nature. What impressed him the most about the Christian theologians he read "was their certainty . . . that the human condition placed inherent limitations on human possibility. Original sin was one way of saying this, and I had no problem with that doctrine."

During my four years at AEI and the eleven years I worked for Radio Free Europe/Radio Liberty, I saw Kristol many times and occasionally had lunch with him. I cannot say that I was part of his inner circle—or even his outer circle—but we did have many amiable conversations. He always asked me about my family. Kristol—like his friend Daniel Moynihan—worried about the American family. He thought that if the family continued to unravel the United States would be in bad shape.

Reading Kristol's "An Autobiographical Memoir," written when he was 75, I learned that he too had a patron—Sidney Hook. "It was Sidney Hook who came to my rescue," Kristol says, "a practice he made a habit of doing for the rest of my life." In 1953 Hook recommended Kristol to be the editor of a new magazine, *Encounter*. Two decades later Hook persuaded New York University to hire Kristol as a professor. "The appointment," Kristol says, "was largely due to vigorous lobbying by Sidney Hook."

Hook was Kristol's mentor as well as his patron. Hook's "writings revealed to me the power of logical, coherent analysis, something my formal education had neglected." On broad foreign policy questions Kristol and Hook were in agreement. Like Hook, Kristol called himself a Cold Warrior. Like Hook, Kristol argued that Americans who belonged to the American Communist Party should be denied a government job because the Party was controlled by the Soviet Union. "The Communists, after all, were a totalitarian group hostile to our constitutional democracy."

In "Memoirs of a 'Cold Warrior,'" written in 1968, Kristol notes that the term anti-anti-communist was "invented, I think, by Sidney Hook." Kristol ends the essay with a strong defense of anti-communism. "Looking back on the Cold War of the 1950s against Stalinism, . . . it was, by every canon I recognize, a just war, and I am pleased to have had a small part in it."

Twenty-five years later, Kristol became a different kind of cold warrior. In "My Cold War," Kristol's main concern is liberalism, not communism. "It was the fundamental assumptions of contemporary liberalism that were my enemy."

In this uncharacteristically shrill essay, Kristol demonizes liberalism. He speaks of the "rot and decadence germinating within American society—a rot and decadence that was no longer the consequence of liberalism but was the actual agenda of contemporary liberalism." Liberalism is an "ethos that aims at . . . moral anarchy." Liberalism, Kristol says in "The Right Stuff," is a disaster because of its "simplistic views of human nature"; its utopian social philosophy, and its "secularist animus against religion."

I found Kristol's attack on liberalism puzzling. My liberal friends are not utopians—and they are not hostile to religion. Undoubtedly, some liberals are secular humanists, but I know many liberals who are practicing Catholics, Protestants, and Jews.

I also was surprised that Kristol occasionally implies that irreligious people are "anxious empty souls" who lack a strong sense of commitment. Sidney Hook was irreligious but he was not an anxious empty soul. Moreover, he had a strong commitment to the defense of liberty. Kristol doesn't make a clear distinction between irreligion, which is increasing in the United States, and secular humanism. Irreligious people are not necessarily hostile to religion; secular humanists are. Secular humanists often want to ban any mention of God in the public sphere.

Though Kristol worried about secular humanism, he argued in 1991 that secular humanism was waning. "If one looks back at the intellectual history of this century, one sees the rational religion of secular humanism gradually losing its credibility." Secular humanism was waning in part because of the rise of "Christian political conservatism," which Kristol also calls "populist conservatism."

Kristol worried more generally about the decline in religious observance. He notes that "all political philosophers prior to the twentieth century, regardless of their personal piety or lack thereof, understood the importance of religion in the life of the political community." Yet he neglects to point out that these same political philosophers warned about the dangers of religious zealotry, which often led to violent civil discord.

Kristol was not sure what to make of Christian political conservatism. He says it may pose a threat to America's political stability. "It is not at all unimaginable that the United States is headed for a bitter and sustained *Kulturkampf* that could overwhelm conventional notions of what is and what is not political." But he also says that Christian populist conservatism "could turn out to be 'the last best hope' of contemporary conservatism."

I sometimes daydream of having lunch again with Kristol so that I could ask him:"Don't you think you should have been more critical of Christian populist conservatism?" I might mention a political survey conducted by the American Enterprise Institute in which a majority of evangelical Christians agreed with the statement: "The American way of life is disappearing so fast that we may have to use force to save it."

Kristol would not have been annoyed by my question. I suspect he would say to me what he says in the last paragraph of his memoir: "But my personal opinion is hardly authoritative, and I am well aware that the unanticipated consequences of ideas and acts are often very different from what was originally attended."

Though I disagree with Kristol's analysis of religion in American life, I agree with his negative view of the counterculture and I agree with the main tenets of neoconservatism, which he said "is not at all hostile to the idea of a welfare state." Neoconservatives, he continues, are for "some form of national health insurance, [and] some kind of family assistance plan." Neoconservatism "has great respect . . for the power of the market to respond efficiently to economic realities while preserving the maximum degree of individual freedom."

I agree with Kristol on many questions, but Kristol was more than the sum of his ideas. One could say he was a charismatic figure—how else explain his influence? One could also say that he was charming.

"So here I am and here we are," Kristol says on the final pages of his memoir. "I conclude this memoir on my seventh-fifth birthday and a few days after our fifty-third wedding anniversary." He is a happily married man who is close to his two children who are "intellectually and politically congenial." Kristol's self-satisfaction smacks of gratitude, not smugness.

I am not "theotropic," which is what Kristol called himself, yet Kristol did influence my approach to intellectual life. What I learned from my acquaintance with him is that one should strive to be serious but not solemn, that one should be intellectually engaged but also detached, and that one should not take oneself too seriously.

The last time I saw Kristol—about a year before he died—was at an AEI conference. He greeted me by smiling and saying, "I'm still here."

CHAPTER 7

Resident Fellow:
American Enterprise Institute

(Job #24)

Irving Kristol remembers that when he was in his late twenties he was invited to a cocktails-and-buffet party at the apartment of William Phillips, the editor of *Partisan Review*. After getting a plate of food and sitting down on the sofa, he realized that on his right was Mary McCarthy and on his left Hannah Arendt—and facing him in a chair was Diana Trilling. "I was trapped," he says, "and remember thinking, as I sank into terrified paralysis of body and mind, that this was an event to remember."

In the 1940s and 1950s McCarthy and Arendt were leading American intellectuals. McCarthy was known mainly for her essays, and Arendt was known for her influential book, *The Origins of Totalitarianism*. Diana Trilling, the wife of Lionel Trilling, was also a well-known essayist.

When I was having lunch during my first week at the American Enterprise Institute, I felt roughly the same way Kristol felt at that party. I was sitting in a lunchroom with a sandwich I had bought from a local takeout—this was before AEI put in a posh dining room—and around the table was a retired Yale Professor of Economics, a future Supreme Court Justice, and a future UN Ambassador. The economist was William J. Fellner, who had been a member of President Nixon's and Ford's Council of Economic Advisers; the future Supreme Court Justice was Antonin Scalia; and the future UN Ambassador was Jeane Kirkpatrick. I just sat and listened.

In my first two years at AEI I don't recall having an extended conversation with either Fellner or Scalia but I did have many conversations with Kirkpatrick, who invited my wife and me to her house for dinner, where we met the Washington correspondent for a leading Italian newspaper. I remember other dinner parties with prominent neocons, including an AEI dinner— tuxedo required—where my wife and I sat next to David Brooks, who had not yet become a *New York Times* columnist.

Because I was a resident fellow at AEI, I received many invitations to lunches and dinners. I had dinner at The Palm—a Washington restaurant frequented by lobbyists and politicians—with R. Emmett Tyrell (the editor of *The American Spectator*) and Elliott Abrams, who worked for Senator Moynihan and would go on to serve in many Republican administrations. I had dinner with the Advisory Board of the *American Scholar*, where I sat next to a leading sociologist, Edward Shils, who taught at the University of Chicago and Cambridge University. I had dinner with William Bennett, who would become head of the Department of Education under Ronald Reagan.

I had lunch in New York with Neal Kozodoy, the executive editor of *Commentary*. On another trip to New York I had lunch with Midge Decter, the wife of *Commentary* editor Norman Podhoretz. Decter, who worked for Basic Books, was interested in the book I was working on: *Special Interest Groups in American Politics*.

What a dramatic change in my life! Five years earlier I was about to take a job sorting mail in the Post Office. Now I was a fellow at AEI, a prestigious—at least in neocon circles—think tank. In February 1979 *Esquire* listed me as a young member of the Neoconservative Establishment. In December 1981 the *New York Times Magazine* quoted me in an article about Kristol.

In December 1980 I got a letter from E. Pendleton James, the

Director of Presidential Personnel for President-elect Ronald Reagan. "As you know, you have been suggested for consideration for a position in the Reagan Administration. . . . Although we cannot predict when we might be in touch, please be assured that you will be seriously considered as we seek the most qualified team to serve President-elect Reagan after he takes office in January." I have no idea what James was referring to when he said "as you know." Nothing came of it, but I was flattered to be considered for a job in the Reagan administration.

Kristol said to me that at AEI I should be "writing, writing, writing." During my first two years there I wrote a lot—essays and reviews for several magazines as well as several op-ed pieces for the *Washington Post*. I wrote "The Constitution and the Spirit of Commerce" for a collection of essays on the Constitution edited by AEI constitutional scholar Robert Goldwin; I wrote "The Idea of Equality in American Literature" for a book of essays on capitalism edited by the sociologist Peter Berger.

I was in demand—sought out by editors and also by young neocons who wanted advice about how to get published. I felt as if I had won the lottery or a quiz show jackpot.

Being a Resident Fellow at AEI was not exactly a job. I had no boss and no responsibilities; I could come and go as I pleased. But I did worry about what I would do after my two-year fellowship was up. I never felt that AEI would keep me on, since I was neither an economist nor a political scientist. Kristol was not an economist or political scientist, but I could not compare myself to Kristol. He was an influential writer and editor, and he was a professor at New York University.

But for the most part my first two years at AEI were enjoyable. I read many writers who defended capitalism, including Adam Smith, though he never used the word capitalism, which is a nineteenth-century coinage. I was drawn to Adam Smith because of my interest in eighteenth-century British literature, which began in college when I took a course on Samuel Johnson with Paul Fussell. *The Public Interest* published my essay, "Adam Smith and the Commercial Republic." A year later AEI reprinted it as a pamphlet.

I wrote about Smith in the book I worked on at AEI, *Special Interest Groups in American Politics*. Kristol liked my book, and he wrote an elegant forward to it. The book, which ended up being published by Transaction Books, was reviewed favorably by *Choice*, which called it "an interesting and intellectually appealing analysis defending the role of interest groups in American politics." What was most gratifying, aside from Kristol's praise, was a letter from the intellectual historian John Diggins, who wrote to me that my book was a "splendid job."

When I finished the book, I felt a sense of accomplishment—my first book! Yet I also was surprised that I had written it. I had never taken a course in American history or in political theory. Wasn't I wandering far afield from literary and cultural studies? But the theoretical core of the book was about ideas that flourished in the British Enlightenment, a subject that I would return to again twenty years later, when I wrote a book about Enlightenment thought.

Recently, I checked on the Internet to see how *Special Interest Groups in American Politics* was doing. I learned that on two websites the author of the book is named Steven I. Miller. Not my name! Because of my exceedingly common name, I'm often listed as the author of books that I did not write. I have prayed to the God of Disambiguation, but to no avail. If you look up Stephen Miller you will find a half-dozen authors with that name.

Many years later I wrote a short article about my name problem, which continues to bedevil me.

When I sit down with old friends who, like me, are in their 70s, I sometimes ask: "If you could live your life again, would you do anything differently?" Most just scratch their heads and say, "I dunno." Recently, I told three old friends that I would do one thing differently: I would get a middle initial—either Q or X—to distinguish myself from the many Stephen Millers who write books. Or I would give myself a full middle name—say, Xavier or Quentin.

In my youth and middle age, my very common name—the White Pages lists 98 Stephen Millers in Virginia, but I bet there are more— was only a minor problem at airports and department stores. At least four times, I heard a request for Stephen Miller to please come to the reservation desk or information counter. It always turned out to be another Stephen Miller; but I would get a shot of adrenaline every time I heard my name, thinking that something terrible had happened to someone in my family.

I also endured the weak jokes of innumerable sales clerks, who would say to me, "So, are you the Steve Miller of the Steve Miller band?" To which I responded sarcastically, "Yeah, right." And once I got a 1099 Tax Statement for Miscellaneous Income from a newspaper, although that year I hadn't written anything for it. I contacted them about the mistake, but they never replied. I didn't feel like trying to straighten this out (it was a small amount), so on that year's tax return I listed income that I had never received for an article that I had never written.

The misattribution problem did not become serious until 2006, when I published Conversation: A History of a Declining Art. *First, several letters addressed to me care of Yale University Press were sent to another Stephen Miller published by Yale: a distinguished classicist who writes on ancient Greek athletics. Second, on many bookstore websites, I was wrongly described as the author of two biographies and several historical novels.*

My corpus of misattributed books got much larger after the publication of my actual latest book, Walking New York: Reflections of American Writers from Walt Whitman to Teju Cole. *Walmart was selling this book, but it incorrectly listed me as the author of* Sweet Blonde, *a biography of Dolly Parton. And I soon found out that on the websites of many independent bookstores, I am described in the following way: "Stephen Miller currently teaches courses in Zoology, Biology and Invertebrate Zoology at the College of the Ozarks, Point Lookout, MO (Branson). He is also the author of General Zoology Lab Manual."*

I emailed one bookstore to tell them that I am not a zoologist. They said the information about me was given to them by a central book information service. They could do nothing about it. I got the same response from another independent bookstore. I wrote to my publisher to see if they could do something about the misattribution, but I have not yet received a reply.

Because my book is being sold on websites around the world, the problem of misattribution is not confined to the United States. The list of books attributed to me varies by country. On a Spanish website, I am the author of La Mensajera (The Messenger). On several German websites, I'm the author of a biography of Johnny Cash. On a Dutch website, I am the author of several books, including Hawaii by Sextant *and* Piwik Web Analytics Essentials. *On a Polish website, I'm the author of* From Fat to Fit: The Simple Way to Transform Your Family Health *as well as* Starting and Running a Sandwich-Coffee Bar.

On many websites in Europe and Asia, I have a middle initial: H. How did the H get there when the name on the book jacket is Stephen Miller?

Is this misattribution a joke being played on me by the shade of Jorge Luis Borges or Franz Kafka? I can see myself as a character in a short story who is trying to find the Transnational Ministry of Author Information, which is located either in a castle in Transylvania or in a strip mall in suburban Los Angeles. If I ever get in touch with these incompetent bureaucrats, I will say, "I want to be disambiguated. Now!"

I could construct my own website, but one already exists. If you Google "Stephen Miller Author," you will find a website: stephenmillerwriter.com. The Author's Official Website. But this is not me. The same author also has stephenmillerwriter.org. My website would have to include my birth date in the address.

Lately I have begun to wonder if I should be so concerned about misattribution. Perhaps being described as the author of a wide variety of books is good for sales. I can see a would-be reader saying, "This guy is amazing. He is a scientist and a literary guy—a renaissance man!" So maybe I should say: Let a Thousand Misattributions

Bloom. But often I daydream of publishing a book under the name of Stephen X. Miller.

A few years before *Special Interest Groups in American Politics* appeared, the essayist Joseph Epstein gave me a few words of advice. "Having read a good deal of your work by now, I have a single notion about it: if I were to give you advice à la an agent, it would be to pick my subjects most carefully. I think, in other words, that you have reached a point where you can write well about almost anything—but my point is—why write about anything?"

I was flattered that Epstein, whose writing I admired, was giving me advice—good advice—but I didn't take it. I cannot explain why I have continued to write about a wide variety of subjects. People ask me why I chose to write X and I don't know the answer. I can only say I get a sort of intellectual itch about a subject that I have to scratch—that is, I have to write about the subject in order to clarify my thoughts about it. But there is some continuity in my writing: I've written many essays about eighteenth-century British writers and many essays about commerce and culture—or, rather, what writers have said about commerce.

Why have so many writers looked down on people who are—as the British put it—in trade? In an essay written when I was at AEI I argued that disdain for commerce is what might be called a topos—a recurrent theme in Western literature. In the *Odyssey*, a Phaeacian thinks Odysseus is a trader because Odysseus declines to participate in an athletic competition. In the Homeric world, traders lack athletic prowess. Odysseus is furious. To be called a trader is an insult because traders are greedy, deceitful, and cowardly. "Your slander fans the anger in my heart!" Odysseus says.

In an essay written many years later, I noted that Greek, Roman, and early Christian writers often argued that a desire for profit is an insatiable desire. Taking a cue from Aristotle, Thomas Aquinas said that "trade, insofar as it aims at making profits, is most reprehensible, since the desire for gain knows no bounds but reaches into the infinite."

It was not until the early eighteenth century that some English writers began to challenge the traditional view of commerce. In the *Spectator*, which began publication in 1711, Joseph Addison defended merchants. "There are not more useful members in a commonwealth than merchants. They knit mankind together in a mutual intercourse of good offices, distribute the gifts of nature, find work for the poor, add wealth to the rich, and magnificence to the great."

Addison made a radical suggestion: English aristocrats, who often led idle lives, should emulate the Jews and become industrious men of commerce. Jews, Addison says, have greatly benefited humankind because they are traders: "They are, indeed, so disseminated through all the trading parts of the world, that they are become the instruments by which the most distant nations converse with one another and by which mankind are knit together in a general correspondence."

Samuel Johnson agreed with Addison about the benefits of commerce. In Johnson's view, a commercial society gives more opportunity for the poor to better their condition: "To entail irreversible poverty upon generation after generation only because the ancestor happened to be poor is in itself cruel, if not unjust, and is wholly contrary to the maxims of a commercial nation."

Most 18th-century English writers, however, had a negative view of commerce. They argued that commercial expansion depopulates the countryside, undermines morality, and weakens public-spiritedness. Most 19th- and 20th-century English poets and essayists also took a dark view of commerce. Deploring the growth of commerce, John Ruskin said that "the ruling goddess [of Britain] may be best generally described as the 'Goddess of Getting-On' or 'Britannia of the Market.'" According to Ruskin, commerce had ruined the minds of Englishmen: "It is simply and sternly impossible for the English public, at the moment, to understand any thoughtful writing—so incapable of thought has it become in its insanity of avarice."

American writers have not been as hostile to commerce as English writers. "Many of our most valuable public men have been merchants," said Washington Irving. According to Walt Whitman, America was destined for a "grander future" than Europe, in part because of "the complicated business genius . . . of Americans." In his journals, Ralph Waldo Emerson said that "we rail at trade, but the historian of the world will see that it was the principle of liberty; that it settled America, and destroyed feudalism, and made peace and keeps peace; that it will abolish slavery."

William Dean Howells found ambitious American businessmen interesting. Reminiscing about his first trip to New York, Howells wrote that, on the ferry, "I had the company of a young New-Yorker, whom I had met on the boat coming down, and who was of the light, hopeful, adventurous business type which seems peculiar to the city, and which has always attracted me." The hero in *The Rise of Silas Lapham* (1885) is a self-made man who became wealthy by manufacturing high-quality paint. "Make Lapham vulgar but not sordid," Howells wrote in his notebook. Lapham is an honest businessman, though he gets into financial trouble when a former partner browbeats him into buying risky securities.

Yet Howells disliked thinking about the commercial aspects of being a writer. In "The Man of Letters as Man of Business," he says that among writers "the instinctive sense of the dishonor which money-purchase does to art is so strong that sometimes a man of letters who can pay his way otherwise refuses pay for his work, as Lord Byron did, for a while, from a noble pride." A shrewd negotiator with publishers, Howells was one of the most commercially successful American novelists, yet he frequently attacked commerce in his essays. New York was ugly, dirty, noisy, and smelly because it was "the commercial metropolis."

There are sympathetic portraits of businessmen in novels by Abraham Cahan, Theodore Dreiser, F. Scott Fitzgerald, and Sinclair Lewis; yet after World War II, most American literary writers painted the business world in dark colors. In 1978, John Gardner complained that most contemporary American writers preached "a whining hatred of American business."

After I finished *Special Interest Groups in American Politics* my two-year fellowship at AEI was up. If I wanted to stay at AEI, I had to raise funds to pay my salary, which I did. The Twentieth Century Fund, a nonprofit foundation based in New York, commissioned me to write a book on the National Endowment for the Humanities, so now I could stay at AEI for another two years.

Before working on that book, I chaired a conference at AEI on commerce and culture. I don't remember much about the one-day conference except that some well-known figures in the cultural world attended. I also remember that the keynote speaker was Allan Bloom, a professor at the University of Chicago. Six years later he would write the best-selling *The Closing of the American Mind.*

I did not know Bloom, but he was a close friend of Walter Berns, who was the person I knew best at AEI. Both had studied with the philosopher Leo Strauss at the University of Chicago and both had taught at Cornell and the University of Toronto. Berns persuaded me to make Bloom the keynote speaker.

I remember very little about Bloom's lecture, which was about Flaubert. What I do remember was that he smoked a cigarette while he talked—this was before there were no smoking rules—and I watched with fascination as the ash from his cigarette grew longer. I wondered when he would tap his cigarette in an ashtray.

I tried to pay attention to what Bloom was saying but I couldn't. He talked a lot about Flaubert and modernity. Modernity was a favorite word with the Straussians.

Strauss was greatly admired—I would say almost worshiped—by many neocons, including several at AEI. Kristol says: "Encountering Strauss's work produced the intellectual shock that is a once-in-a-lifetime experience. He turned one's intellectual experience upside down." I read two books by Strauss, but I found him idiosyncratic in his approach to philosophical texts. Perhaps I did not work hard enough to understand him.

When I first arrived at AEI I thought modernity was the same thing as modernism, a movement in the arts that began in the first decade of the twentieth century. But then I learned that the Straussians thought modernity began with Machiavelli.

Modernity is a word that many writers like to use but it is often not clear what it means. A recent biographer of Chaucer says that Chaucer "understood the drive to criticize modernity." She seems to imply that modernity means a predominantly commercial society. Some writers associate modernity with the early twentieth century. "Modernity is alienating, and it has been alienating for a great while," says Andrew Solomon in the *New Yorker*.

Modernity is a notion that is very hard to pin down. So is post-modernism. I wrestled with the meaning of this word when I was writing "Are We Living in a Postmodern Age?" which appeared in a magazine published by AEI. After finishing this piece, which looks at the various meanings of postmodern, I decided that the word post-modern should be put in the bin of WORDS AND PHRASES TO BE AVOIDED. They include existential, dialectic, late capitalist, and— my favorite—hermeneutical.

At first it was a relief to work on a book about the National Endowment for the Humanities. I was glad to get away from writing and talking about commerce and culture, modernity and postmod-ernism. I was now for the first time in my life doing policy research, since I was supposed to make recommendations for improving the National Endowment for the Humanities. But there was a major downside to this project. I was not an independent author; I was un-der contract to the Twentieth Century Fund, which paid my salary.

In the second year of the project the contract stipulated that I would be paid after I completed a third of the book and the work was approved by the Fund. I am a disciplined writer who has never been late for a deadline. I handed in one/third of the book on schedule, but a month went by and there was no check in the mail. If I didn't get paid soon I would be in deep water financially, so I called the Fund and was told that the director of the Twentieth Century Fund had not yet gotten round to reading my chapters.

"I don't give a damn about when the director reads it," I yelled. "I need that money now. Do you want me to sue you for breach of contract?" The check arrived three days after I made the call.

A few years later, at a meeting of freelance writers, I met a man who also had written a book under contract to the Twentieth Century Fund.

"Did you sue them?" he asked me.

"No, I didn't."

"I did," he said. "Everyone I know who has done a book for the Fund has sued them."

The Fund also gave me a hard time on editorial matters. It wanted me to remove some passages in the book that the director thought were too critical of NEH. I resisted but the Fund paid my salary so I could not resist too much. Had I written this book as an independent author, I would have been more critical of NEH.

Moreover, I would not have entitled the book *Excellence & Equity: The National Endowment for the Humanities*. It should have been entitled *Excellence or Equity*. In my view a preoccupation with equity undermines the support of excellence. What does equity mean but a proportional distribution of grants?

Forty years after having written this book, I read George Will's comment that equity is "Washington's word du jour. . . . This word implies, without defining, a social outcome different from—and superior to—the equality affirmed in the Declaration of Independence and the Constitution's guarantee of equal protection of the laws." I wonder: Did I play some small role in making equity a word du jour?

Though I found writing the NEH book for the most part a chore, I enjoyed reading the *Congressional Record* on microfilm in order to look at the dance of legislation. NEH turned out to be very different from what scholars in the humanities had hoped for. According to Charles Blitzer, who in 1965 was the Executive Director of the American Council of Learned Societies, "the proper sister of the humanities endowment is the National Science Foundation and not the National Endowment for the Arts." He added that the comparison with the arts is inappropriate, since "the arts by definition, presuppose an audience in a way that the humanities do not." That was not the view of Senator Pell, who thought NEH should spend most of its funds on programs for the general public.

I also thought about the question of representativeness. In a report to Congress in 1980 NEH chairman Joseph Duffey claimed that "the effort to broaden representation on panels by women and minorities had been successful. Next year, no panel will have less than one-third women, and most panels will have 50 percent." How do we gauge representativeness? The number of women awarded doctorates in the humanities varies greatly by discipline. In art history more women than men are awarded doctorates. In 1975 sixty-five doctorates were awarded to men in art history and 101 to women. By contrast, in philosophy more men than women are awarded doctorates. According to the American Council of Learned Societies, "the share of women earning doctorates in philosophy fluctuated in the 24–30% range for most of the 1990s and the first decade of the 21st century."

Thus a peer review panel on art history would be representative if it were two/thirds women whereas a peer review panel in philosophy would be representative if it were roughly one/third women. In a public letter to NEH Sidney Hook complained that the agency was setting numerical goals in the selection of reviewers.

Duffey may have hoped that "representative" panels would result in a "representative" distribution of grants, but this is a faulty assumption—and, to my mind, an insidious assumption because it assumes that a woman philosopher is more likely to award a grant to a woman applicant. I argued that "the primary allegiance of a scholar is to his discipline, not to his sex or race."

In the course of writing this book I talked to many scholars in the humanities. The most preeminent was Sir Isaiah Berlin, who was head of the British Council, an organization that gives grants to scholars in the humanities. I wrote to him and he agreed to see me for an hour at the Athenaeum Club in London. I asked him: "What if a delegation of Scotsmen came to see you and said Scotsmen had not received a representative percentage of grants?"

Isaiah Berlin smiled: "I would tell them to find more intelligent Scotsmen."

When *Excellence & Equity* was published, I was deeply involved in my new job and not particularly interested in the fate of the book. The review in the *Washington Times* by Ronald Berman, the former chairman of NEH, was the most negative. He concludes: "There is not much reason to have confidence in this book. It was, I think, written in a hurry and it leaves out most of what we would like to know. What it includes—sententious, moralistic, pseudo-critical—is not much help." By contrast, Alvin C. Eurich, who had been vice president of the Aspen Institute for Humanistic studies, wrote in *Book Forum*: "This is an excellent book, well worth reading by anyone interested in the humanities, exceedingly well documented and written."

In my view *Excellence & Equity* was not as bad as Berman said and not as good as Eurich said.

When I got my last check from the Twentieth Century Fund, I realized that my days at AEI were numbered. I was told by the AEI chairman that I could stay on at AEI if I found a foundation to pay my salary, but I knew that was impossible. I had no book project that would interest a foundation.

After a ten-year hiatus, I was in the job market again. The rollercoaster was going down.

I hoped that looking for a job would be easier now than it was ten years ago, but my phone didn't ring with job offers. What did I have to offer a potential employee? I had an erratic career—journalist, academic, bureaucrat. I was a decent writer, but the only kind of writing that is marketable is public relations or speechwriting, and I had never done either. I would have liked to be an editor for a highbrow magazine but those jobs are few and far between.

I did get two interviews out of the blue—one to work on Senator Daniel Moynihan's staff, the other to work for the Heritage Foundation. I thought the Moynihan interview—I only saw his staff—went well, but I never heard back from them. The interview with the Heritage Foundation went badly. The interviewer asked my position on abortion. I found the question irritating. "I'm supposed to write about cultural policy, so why do you want to know my position on aboriton?" I was not offered a job, which didn't upset me because I disliked the Heritage Foundation. At Heritage I would not be free to write as I pleased; most staffers were told what to write.

Things were looking bleak when suddenly a job was dangled before me: Special Assistant to James Buckley, the newly appointed President of Radio Free Europe/Radio Liberty. Buckley was a former senator from New York (in 1976 he had been defeated by Moynihan). The idea for this job came from Ben Wattenberg, an AEI Fellow who wrote a best-selling book with Richard M. Scammon, *The Real Majority: An Extraordinary Examination of the American Electorate.* Wattenberg had been appointed Vice-Chairman of the Board for International Broadcasting (BIB), which oversaw Radio Free Europe/ Radio Liberty, and he wanted someone he could trust to give him an accurate account of what was happening at RFE/RL. Wattenberg, I assume, persuaded Buckley that I would be useful to him. I had to pass muster with Frank Shakespeare, the chairman of BIB. Shakespeare had been head of the United States Information Agency under Nixon and before that president of CBS Television. After a brief interview with Shakespeare, I learned that the job was mine. I started in January 1983.

RFE/RL was headquartered in Munich, but I worked in the Washington office, which was a five minute walk from AEI, so I occasionally went to AEI to hear a lecture or have lunch with a former AEI colleague. The person I saw most frequently was Walter Berns. Walter was a very cultivated man who had a dry sense of humor. He once told me that his daughter wished he would stop writing books defending unpopular positions—e.g. *For Capital Punishment: Crime and the Morality of the Death Penalty*. I thought the arguments he advanced in this book were persuasive but he was swimming against a very strong current. I always enjoyed talking to Walter and reading his work. Though he studied under Leo Strauss, his writing is more lucid and elegant than Strauss's. Walter did not talk in high-flown abstractions. I don't recall him ever using the word modernity. We mostly talked about novels. I remember talking to him about Dickens, Trollope, and George Eliot. I also saw Walter outside AEI. My wife and I were invited to his apartment for dinner, and we invited them to our house.

Our friendship came to an end after I published "Confessions of a Rootless Cosmopolitan Jew." It appeared in *First Things* and was reprinted in a collection of essays entitled *The Chosen People in an Almost Chosen Nation: Jews and Judaism in America*.

Many neocons disliked this essay. The editor of *Commentary* sent me a note saying: Re "Confessions" ?????" A former colleague of mine at AEI was so incensed by my essay that he wrote a letter to the editor in which he accused me of being a hypocrite for putting my mother in a Jewish nursing home even though I was not a practicing Jew. Being in a Jewish nursing home was my mother's choice. It had nothing to do with me.

Walter, who was a practicing Episcopalian, never told me what he thought of my article, but at an AEI reception his wife asked me: "Why did you publish this article? These are thoughts that I would put in my diary."

"I don't keep a diary," I said politely. "When I write something, I write it for publication."

I rarely reread what I've written but recently I decided to reread this essay. I have two regrets. I think the choice of words that I used for the title was a mistake. I knew that "rootless cosmopolitan" was an anti-Semitic expression in Russia—one that Stalin used—but I was trying to say it is also a useful phrase to describe secular American Jews like myself—Jews who have married gentiles and lost touch with the Jewish community. I should have said: "Confessions of an Unaffiliated Jew."

I also regret having written the following two sentences. "No doubt, if all Jews followed in my footsteps, the Jewish people would no longer exist. My response to that is: "So what?" I wrote "So what?" because I objected to the expression "Silent Holocaust," which is sometimes used to describe what happens when Jews marry Christians and let their children be raised as non-Jews. I now think the words "So what?" are harsh; they make me sound hostile to Judaism, which is not the case.

In my essay I note that my parents were secular Jews who never went to a synagogue though we did celebrate Hanukkah and Passover, so it is not surprising that I didn't have a strong attachment to Judaism. The essay is an effort to describe my complex feelings about my Jewish heritage. Nowhere in the essay do I suggest that my unaffiliated secular life is a path for others to follow.

CHAPTER 8

Special Assistant to the President of Radio Free Europe/Radio Liberty

(Job # 25)

I liked the idea of working for Radio Free Europe/Radio Liberty because many historians and journalists praised what RFE/RL was doing. According to the historian Walter Laqueur, "these Munich-based stations provided a free flow of information to the East and contributed more than any other Western source to the . . . erosion of Soviet ideology."

The task I was first assigned at RFE/RL was a difficult one: make recommendations for improving it. Seven weeks after I started to work I gave a preliminary report to James Buckley, whom I met in London, where RFE/RL had a news bureau. Before meeting Buckley, I spent three weeks in Munich, where RFE/RL was headquartered.

My three weeks in Munich were a whirlwind of meals and meetings. Many staffers were eager to tell me what was wrong with RFE/RL and how it should be fixed. I wanted to make sure that I did not jump to conclusions. I always kept in mind the saying: "If it's not broke, don't fix it."

I knew it would not be easy to evaluate RFE/RL, which is a

collection of semi-autonomous language services. In 1983 it had twenty language services—six language services in Radio Free Europe and fourteen in Radio Liberty.

Many people confuse RFE/RL with the Voice of America. The latter is the official U.S. government radio station, so it not only provides news but also reflects the views of the current administration. RFE/RL does not reflect the government's views. Its main focus is on internal developments in the countries to which it broadcasts. RFE/RL does not have central scripting. By contrast, the Voice of America's scripts are written in English and translated into the many languages it broadcasts in.

RFE/RL's twenty language services have one constraint: for their hourly fifteen-minute news segments they have to select items from a "budget" of news provided by RFE/RL's news bureau.

How did I go about evaluating the twenty different language services? I read scripts that RFE/RL's management randomly selected to be translated. I read reports that were written by academics who listened to a week's worth of programming. I also read reports from RFE/RL's pollster about the listeners to the various services. Soviet bloc leaders clearly worried about the impact of RFE/RL because they frequently tried to jam its broadcasts; sometimes it was difficult for listeners to hear a program.

The different services varied widely in quality. The Polish Service was considered by many to be outstanding. Its contributors included leading Polish writers from Poland and abroad. (The head of the Polish Service wrote a highly-regarded biography of Joseph Conrad.) Describing Poland during the Solidarity strikes in 1980, the historian Timothy Garton Ash said that the "workers and their intellectual advisers sit drafting texts, listening to the latest news from Radio Free Europe on a short-wave transistor radio."

In general, I was impressed by RFE/RL staffers. (One staffer became the president of Estonia.) Though I felt that some staffers disdained me because I was a Reagan Administration appointee, other staffers welcomed me because they hoped Buckley would make the language services take a harder line on communist regimes.

I don't think anyone at RFE/RL was pro-communist, but some RFE/RL staffers thought the best that could be achieved in Soviet bloc countries was what Hungary had achieved—a regime that tolerated dissenters so long as they did not call for the overthrow of the communist government. Staffers who took this review were reluctant to give airtime to dissidents who called for democracy. In their view dissident thinkers were utopian—and counterproductive. My own view was that the dissidents should be given airtime.

Because I did know any of the languages RFE/RL broadcast in, I could not listen to live programming. But I did read the news budget, which included news in English, French, and German. When I met Buckley in London, I told him that the spectrum of news and opinion in the news budget was too narrow. The news budget focused on Western Europe. Many staffers were Euro-centered; they thought developments in Western Europe interested listeners far more than developments in the United States. I argued that people in the Soviet bloc were interested in the United States, so there should be more news and opinion about the United States.

Buckley agreed with my recommendations and gave me the task of putting more news about the United States in the news budget. I hired three journalists to write articles about American life. The venture was not successful because many language services did not use the articles the three journalists wrote. After two years the three journalists left for other jobs and were not replaced. My effort to increase the news about the United States was not a total failure, however, because the news budget now included more news about the U.S. as well as a wider spectrum of political opinion.

My main job in the Washington office was vetting candidates for jobs at RFE/RL. Buckley agreed with most of my recommendations. It was a pleasure to work for him, though I didn't see him very often since he lived in Munich. He was a dedicated public servant who listened carefully to whatever I said about RFE/RL.

Buckley must have found it difficult to run RFE/RL. There were so many factions in Munich. In almost every language service there were squabbles between different generations of staffers. There were also minor brouhahas. One summer an American scholar who was doing research at RFE/RL's archives was upset about a program on South Africa that he had heard on the Polish Service. The researcher wrote a memo about the program to the director of the Polish Service, who complained to the head of RFE/RL that this researcher had no right to comment on the Polish Service's programs. Buckley asked me to see what I could do to resolve this dispute. I told the researcher that if he didn't stay out of RFE/RL's internal affairs, he would lose his research privileges. He complied.

The major dispute I handled was about the Russian Service. A handful of staffers and independent observers said that some programs on the Russian Service were anti-democratic and anti-Semitic. A congressional committee investigated the allegations and found no evidence of anti-democratic or anti-Semitic broadcasts. An investigation by the General Accounting Office came back with the same verdict, though it did call for more controls over broadcast content. But the controversy refused to go away. A Democratic congressman from Florida made the same charges. A Russian dissident wrote a report for Helsinki Watch accusing the Russian Service of airing programs that were hostile to pluralism and democracy.

Buckley asked me to look into the question, so I had to read up on contemporary Russian political thought. I told Buckley that the scripts in question were about relatively obscure historical issues that did not lend themselves to easy clarification, I said the scripts were not anti-democratic or anti-Semitic. However, I was told by some Russian Service staffers who were Jewish that I didn't understand that certain code words referred to Jews. In other words, I had to know Russian to fully understand what was going on. They had a point.

I occasionally briefed Ben Wattenberg, the AEI Senior Fellow who had created this job for me, and I attended the Board for International Broadcasting's annual meeting in Munich. The Board had several distinguished members, but it was dominated by Frank Shakespeare, who rarely gave anyone else a chance to talk. Once Shakespeare invited high-level journalists from the New York media to a lunch at Twenty-One, a posh New York restaurant, in order to talk about what RFE/RL was doing. Unfortunately, he spent most of his time praising board members.

I also gave talks about the Radios to American audiences. In my talks I always stressed that the RFE/RL was similar to National Public Radio—and that many distinguished writers participated in its programs. I usually quoted Václav Havel's remark: "If my fellow citizens knew me before I became president [of the Czech Republic], they did so because of these stations."

The reception I got varied. At a New England college the audience seemed hostile. A professor who spoke to me after the lecture accused RFE/RL of broadcasting Cold War propaganda. I told him that RFE/RL doesn't preach to listeners about the evils of communism, for the listeners know what life is like in a communist dictatorship.

The response was different when I talked to an American Legion chapter in a small town in Delaware. This was a very informal affair— a 15 minute talk after I had dinner with them. These men seemed interested in what I had to say. One asked me about jamming. Another asked me how RFE/RL conducted its listenership surveys. A third asked me if I thought East European communist regimes would collapse.

Looking back in my three years working as a Special Assistant, I think my advice helped to improve RFE/RL but only marginally. Nevertheless, I enjoyed the job because I met many interesting people: journalists, academics, writers. RFE/RL often held conferences about the Soviet bloc that attracted leading Soviet scholars, including Adam Ulam, who wrote many books about Russian and Soviet history, and Robert Conquest, the author of books about Stalin's terror and the 1930s famine in Ukraine. I met Peter Reddaway, who wrote about Soviet dissidents. Reddaway wrote that "there is no more important aspect of Western policy towards the Soviet Union than foreign radio broadcasts."

Russian dissident writers often wrote scripts for the Radios. I remember meeting Vladimir Bukovsky, Andrei Sinyavsky, Lyudmila Alexeyeva, Vasily Aksyonov, and Vladimir Voinovich. I became friends with the Yugoslav dissident writer Mihailo Mihailov, who worked for the Russian Service.

I also occasionally met people in the State Department who worked closely with RFE/RL staffers. One turned out to be a Cuban spy. Kendall Myers was arrested in 2009 for spying for Cuba for thirty years, which meant that he started spying around 1970—long after it was clear that Castro was a communist who was supported by the Soviet Union. He was a jovial bear of a man who called me up one day to ask if I could give a lecture on Hungary for the State Department's Foreign Service Institute. I was not an East European scholar, but I agreed.

My job had a secondary benefit: at least a half-dozen trips to Munich, a great city with good food, excellent art museums, and superb classical music concerts. On weekends I occasionally travelled to nearby cities: Augsburg, Nuremberg, Salzburg. I once spent a day at the Tegernsee, a beautiful lake resort near the Austrian border. I went one day with an RFE/RL staffer on a cable car up the Zugspitze, the highest mountain in Germany.

When I was in Munich I stayed at a boutique hotel that was about a 20-minute walk to the RFE/RL, which was next to the Englisches Garten, a beautiful park. In warm weather one often saw nudists sunbathing or even walking about the park. One weekend there was a controversy because a naked man had gotten on a tram. City officials drew the line at naked tram riding.

One summer my whole family was with me for eight weeks; we stayed in an apartment RFE/RL gave us. One day we were walking in the Englisches Garten with our eight-year-old daughter when four naked young men and women were strolling towards us. "Daddy, look!" my daughter gasped. I didn't know what to say, so I said: "Let's get something for lunch."

CHAPTER 9

Editor, *Soviet East/ European Report*

(Job #26)

In 1986 James Buckley left Radio Free Europe/Radio Liberty to become a federal judge on the Court of Appeals in Washington. When I learned that he was leaving, I thought of Pirandello's play, *Six Characters in Search of An Author*; I was now a Special Assistant in search of someone to assist. I knew that I could not keep this job, since the new head of RFE/RL would want his own Special Assistant.

Would I have to look for a job again? Was the rollercoaster hurtling down?

Fortunately, a new job was created for me. I became director of the Washington office of RFE/RL's Research Institute. The Research Institute, which had the world's largest collection of dissident writing from the Soviet bloc, was a think tank composed of experts on Soviet bloc countries. RFE/RL broadcasters made use of its monthly reports, but so did many journalists, academics, and independent researchers. After the Soviet Union collapsed, one observer said that RFE/RL had "the best research facilities in the world for covering the demise of the [Soviet] empire."

My main job was spreading the word about the Research Institute's work by publishing a weekly newsletter called *Soviet/East European*

Report, which was a digest of the best articles the Research Institute published. The newsletter was offered free to journalists, policymakers, and academics. The newsletter was not a new product from RFE/RL. For several years a freelancer had put out a monthly report. I turned it into a weekly.

Since I no longer was a high-level RFE/RL official, I no longer had the perks that came with a high-level job. I did not travel to Munich and I did not vet new candidates. Though I had far fewer free lunches and dinners, I was doing what I liked to do most: write. To put out the newsletter, I also had to read a lot—not only what was published by the Research Institute but also articles and books about the Soviet bloc.

An average workday consisted of reading in the morning and writing in the afternoon. I sometimes went to talks by Soviet bloc experts at the Woodrow Wilson International Center for Scholars or the Johns Hopkins University School of Advanced International Studies.

Two days a week I went to the Y to play squash with a man who worked for the Research Institute. One day I smashed him in the face with my racket and his lip was bleeding. After that I became nervous about playing squash.

My squash partner was a former Navy pilot who had a doctorate in international relations. After one match I asked him why he quit the Navy.

"Know what a cold start is?" he asked.

I said I didn't.

"It's when you don't get enough lift when taking off from an aircraft carrier and your aircraft plunges into the ocean. I began to worry about cold starts."

My squash partner soon left RFE/RL to become a professor at a university. I didn't look for another squash partner because the fear of smashing someone with my racquet made me lose interest in squash. I went back to playing tennis, which I hadn't played in two decades.

I enjoyed talking to my squash partner, who was well-informed about Eastern Europe. Washington is often described as a swamp filled with narcissistic self-promoters, but most of the people I've met in Washington have been well-educated men and women who like to think and write about public policy questions.

The head of the Research Institute, who became a good friend when he moved from Munich to Washington, was a Russia expert who had once worked for the C.I.A. He also had a passion for philosophy. In conversation he would often bring up Plato, which he could read in the original. He was not showing off; he thought Plato could help clarify many questions. Fluent in a half-dozen languages, he left RFE/RL to become a freelance translator. When I last saw him, he told me he was translating for Microsoft. Three weeks later he died in a car crash.

I met another Russia expert: Murray Feshbach, a Georgetown University professor who wrote about the Soviet health care system. People who knew little about life in the Soviet Union sometimes praised its universal free medical care, but Feshbach argued that the Soviet healthcare system was a disaster. He told me that a leading heart clinic in Moscow was on the fifth floor of a building without an elevator. He pointed out that in the Soviet Union there was a dire shortage of basic drugs. It was often hard to find aspirin.

Feshbach, who died in January 2019, argued that Russia's health care system did not improve after the Soviet Union collapsed. In 1993 he published *Ecocide in the USSR: Health And Nature Under Siege*. A decade later he published *Russia's Health and Demographic Crises: Policy Implications and Consequences*.

Feshbach's pessimism was warranted. In the past decade life expectancy in Russia has gone up slightly but it is still much lower—especially for males—than life expectancy in Western Europe. In 2018 it was 68 at birth for males whereas for Britain it was 81 at birth. Russian males drink too much and smoke too much. When I was at the Research Institute Gorbachev tried to curtail the production of vodka. Though he had some success in reducing vodka consumption, many Russians began to make *samogon,* the Russian word for moonshine. I also remember reading that some Russians had died after drinking aircraft de-icer.

Long before I started working for RFE/RL I began reading books about Eastern Europe and the Soviet Union. My interest in this part of the world began in the mid-1960s, when I met my future wife, who had emigrated to the United States in November 1948—her family taking what was probably the last train out of Budapest before the Hungarian communists consolidated their power. Talking to her, I learned a great deal about the Stalinist years in Hungary—from 1948 to 1953. During those years many of her relatives and thousands of others were exiled to the countryside to work on farms under harsh conditions. After Stalin died her relatives were released but they were not allowed to live in a major city and their children often were denied a college education. After the Hungarian Revolution these restrictions gradually were lifted.

Though I was especially interested in Hungary, I mostly read books by Russian writers, including Vladimir Nabokov's *Speak, Memory*, Nadezhda Mandelstam's *Hope Against Hope*, Evgenia Ginsburg's *Journey Into the Whirlwind*, Andrei Sinyavsky's *The Makepeace Experiment,* and Alexander Solzhenitsyn's *The Gulag Archipelago.*

During the next twenty years I wrote essays and book reviews about several Russian writers, including a review of Varlam Shalamov's *Kolyma Tales*, which are stories about life in the Gulag of Kolyma. Here is the opening paragraph of my review of Shalamov.

In the fall of 1944 a group of Americans, among them Vice President Henry Wallace and Owen Lattimore of the Office of War Information, paid a visit to the Soviet Far East. Writing about his trip in the December, 1944, issue of National Geographic, *Lattimore praised the Soviet development effort there as roughly comparable to "a combination of the Hudson Bay Co. and T. V. A." He was also favorably impressed by the Soviet commandant. "Both he and his wife have a trained and sensitive interest in art and music, and also a deep sense of civic responsibility."*

The Soviet couple whom Lattimore praised were in charge of a vast Gulag that claimed the lives of more than three million people. Shalamov spent thirteen years in Kolyma; he survived because someone got him a job as a hospital attendant. In my review I quoted the historian Robert Conquest, who noted that more prisoners were executed in one particular camp in Kolyma alone in 1938 than were executed throughout Russia for the whole of the last century of Tsarist rule.

In the late 1980s, when I was putting out *Soviet/East European Report,* I wrote several articles about East European countries. I also wrote an op-ed piece about the Soviet Union and Fairfax County, Virginia! In 1988 the Soviet Peace Committee, a propaganda arm of the Soviet government, was offering the county a 30-foot "peace statue" from a Soviet Georegian sculptor who was also Vice-President of this committee. The proposed statue, entitled "The Wall of Misunderstanding," was hideous. In the *Washington Post* I wrote: "Depicting a Soviet man breaking through a wall, it's heavy-handed kitsch—social realism at its worst."

Even though the State Department said the Soviet Peace Committee was a major arm of the Soviet propaganda apparatus, several Northern Virginia politicians wanted to accept the sculpture, which would have been placed in front of the Reston Regional Library. "If that happens," I wrote, "then Fairfax County will implicitly be endorsing the notion that U.S.-Soviet relations have been based on a misunderstanding, not on serious policy differences."

At a town hall meeting I made the same arguments that I made in my op-ed piece. A month later Fairfax County rejected the statue.

I also wrote an essay entitled "Totalitarianism, Dead and Alive," which appeared in *Commentary* in 1989. I argued that China remained a totalitarian country despite its reforms, and that we should be wary of making a distinction between hard-liners and reformers. "What has remained constant in China is that hardliners have always won out whenever the regime has seemed directly threatened with the loss of power."

In this essay, which appeared two months after the massacre at Tiananmen Square in June 1989, I also said that "totalitarian regimes are much more resistant to fundamental change than any other kind of political order. The recent events in China confirm the soundness of this view."

Thirty years later there still are communist regimes in China, North Korea, Laos, Vietnam, Cuba, and Belarus. Moreover, the governments of most post-communist states are authoritarian regimes that pay only lip service to liberty. And there is Venezuela, which became a dictatorship with the help of Cuban military and security personnel.

The last essay I wrote on foreign policy, "The Benefits of Soviet Breakdown," appeared in the Winter 1992 issue of *Orbis,* a quarterly journal published by the Foreign Policy Research Institute. The article was a mild critique of the Bush administration's fear that the breakup of the Soviet Union would be destabilizing. "The United States should not become alarmist over expressions of Russian nationalism," I said, "since some degree of nationalist sentiment is inevitable. If the West overreacts to legitimate expressions of Russian nationalism, the ultra-nationalists may win converts by arguing that the West hates all things Russian. A Russia governed by ultranationalists would not necessarily be a danger to the West, but it is likely to be a danger to its neighbors."

But I was not pollyanna-ish. I said that "the sudden break-up of one of the world's most powerful empires makes for an unstable and volatile political situation, one that the West may be able to influence only on the margins."

The Assistant Editor at *Orbis* praised my article, saying "it is one of the best-written and most cogent articles we have received in a long while," but I had second thoughts about the article even when I was writing it. I asked myself: Who am I to discuss American policy towards the Soviet Union when I cannot read Russian? (I once tried to learn Russian but quit after one year.) I felt that I was skating on thin ice. When I finished the piece, I vowed that I would never write another article on an East European country.

I never did write another article about Russia but in May 2016 I published an article in the *Weekly Standard* about a famous China-watcher, Simon Leys, who was strongly critical of the adulation many Western writers expressed for Mao and Maoism. Simon Leys was the pen-name of Pierre Ryckmans, a Belgian who taught for many years in Australia. Leys, who wrote in French, English, and Chinese, became interested in China in 1955 when he traveled there as part of a student delegation. He studied Chinese history and culture in Taiwan and Hong Kong. He also talked to refugees, read newspapers from China, and subscribed to China News Analysis. In 1970, Leys moved to Australia, where he taught in Canberra and Sydney.

In the article I said that Leys was appalled by "the spectacular blunders of nearly all the 'contemporary China' specialists." He quoted John King Fairbank, the influential China scholar who taught at Harvard: "The Maoist revolution is, on the whole, the best thing that has happened to the Chinese people in many centuries." Many China scholars, Leys said, knew what was happening in China but were reluctant to condemn Mao's policies. They spoke of "the China difference," arguing that it was wrong to look at China through the lens of Western values; but, wrote Leys, "things happened in Maoist China that were ghastly by any standard of common decency."

I also quoted Leys' remark that "when it comes to Maoism, some members of the French intellectual elite have easily beaten the world record for stupidity." For stupidity about Maoism, the prize should go to the French philosopher Alain Badiou, who wrote, in 1977, "there is only one great philosopher of our time: Mao Zedong." Badiou, who headed the philosophy department at the École Normale Supérieure—the most prestigious institution of higher learning in France—remains a Maoist. Writing in 2009, Leys quoted a letter from a friend who was angry that "criminal Maoist lies manage to endure. ... Look for instance at the popular success now enjoyed by the 'radical' thinker Alain Badiou, who prides himself on being an emeritus defender of the 'Cultural Revolution.'"

In Leys' view, Mao "repeatedly brought the very regime he himself had created to the brink of chaos and destruction." He argued that Mao's China was more totalitarian than Stalin's Soviet Union. The Maoists "invaded the lives of the people in a way that was far more radical and devastating than in the Soviet Union." In Mao's gulag, the "mental pressure" was severe. "By the fall of 1951, 80 percent of all Chinese had had to take part in mass accusation meetings, or to watch organized lynchings and public executions."

Reviewing *No Enemies, No Hatred* (2012), the collected essays of the Nobel Prize-winning Chinese dissident Liu Xiaobo, Leys agreed with Liu that the Chinese authorities "are enforcing a rigorous amnesia of the recent past. The Tiananmen massacre has been entirely erased from the minds of a new generation—while crude nationalism is being whipped up from time to time."

In 1984 Leys wrote that "Mao's mummy" lies in the "huge and grotesque mausoleum in the heart of Peking." More than three decades later, the mausoleum remains the number-one tourist attraction in Beijing, where you pay your respects to the Great Helmsman by filing past the embalmed corpse and then entering a gift shop where you can buy Mao pins, Mao rings, Mao busts, and Mao bracelets.

Can the Chinese leadership ever do away with Mao worship? Not if it wants to remain a Communist state. In 2012, the year Xi Jinping came to power, Leys wrote that "after more than twenty years of 'reform,' the only feature of Maoist ideology that is being unconditionally retained by the Communist Party is the principle of its absolute monopoly over political power."

JAN NOWAK

During my decade at RFE/RL I chatted occasionally with the most impressive person I met in Washington: Jan Novak, the former director of the Polish Service. In 1996 he was awarded the Presidential Medal of Freedom. In the 1980s he was head of the Polish-American Congress, but he still took a strong interest in RFE/RL and often came to its Washington offices. He was a man who radiated steeliness and courtliness. We occasionally talked about his memoir, *Courier from Warsaw,* which an American movie company had optioned. Novak wanted to have a final say on the script, which the company would not agree to, so the project collapsed, but *Kurier,* a Polish movie based on his book, appeared in 2019.

Courier from Warsaw is one of the most powerful memoirs written about World War II. In the Forward Zbigniew Brzezinski says "it will doubtless earn a lasting place in any select shelf of war memoirs." First published in Polish in London in 1978, the memoir circulated underground in Poland in the early 1980s. In 1989 the official Polish edition was published in Warsaw. The English-language version was published in 1982 by Wayne State University Press.

The *New York Times* ran two lengthy reviews of *Courier.* One was by Jan Kott, the Polish drama critic (he was a high school friend of Nowak's). Kott said: "Fast-paced action, unpredictable and sudden reversals, accuracy of technical detail, flawless descriptions of places and interiors make 'Courier from Warsaw' as fascinating and thrilling to read as the best of John Le Carré's novels." The other was by Theodore Shabad, a *Times* foreign correspondent. He called it a "fascinating memoir" and an "important historical document."

Courier from Warsaw covers six years in Nowak's life. When the war started in September 1939 Nowak had recently been awarded a doctorate in economics and was planning to teach economics. Fighting in the Polish Army, he was taken prisoner but escaped and joined the Home Army—the main army of the Polish underground. (There was a much smaller resistance group backed by the Soviet Union.) Nowak notes that the Polish resistance network existed "on a scale unparalleled in any other occupied country."

Nowak worked on many Home Army projects, including putting out disinformation in German to confuse German authorities or undermine the morale of German soldiers. In 1942 the Home Army chose him to become a courier to the London-based Polish government. Nowak had recently learned English from a Scotsman who had escaped from a German prison camp and was hiding out in Poland.

In the Preface to *Courier* Nowak sums up what he did. "I was the eyewitness to the Polish drama in World War II from the perspective of both London and Warsaw. My first secret trip, from Warsaw to Sweden, was taken at the time when Stalin had broken off relations with the Polish government in London. It was the beginning of a game which would lead to the subjugation of Poland by the Soviet Union. My fifth and last journey as a courier ended in England ten days before the Yalta Conference. I was the first eyewitness to, and participant in, the Warsaw Uprising to reach the West." The Warsaw Uprising began on August 1, 1944 and ended on October 2.

Courier from Warsaw describes three harrowing trips that Nowak made. The first was to Sweden, where Nowak provided information to representatives of the London-based Polish government. He got there by stowing away in the coal bin of a ship that was sailing from Gdansk. If Swedish authorities had known that he was actively involved in fighting the Germans, he would have been interned there for the duration of the war. The trip back to Poland—also by ship—could have been a disaster because an informer had told Nazi authorities the names of the Poles who helped Nowak stow away. The Nazis were waiting in Gdansk to arrest him but the Swedish ship changed course and docked in Szczecin. So Nowak escaped arrest.

The second trip was also by boat to Sweden, but this time he went on to Britain by plane. He almost died because he jumped onto the tarmac before the plane had finished taxiing. A ground crew member saw Nowak's legs dangling—Nowak was still attached to his safety belt— and shouted at the pilot to not move the aircraft. "Had the aircraft moved on, I would have broken in half like a match at the very moment when I reached my destination."

Nowak was supposed to parachute back into Poland but on a training jump he seriously injured himself so parachuting was out. After spending six months in London, he flew back to Poland but not directly. It was a five-leg journey: first a stop in Cornwall, then on to Gibraltar, then to Naples, then to a base near Brindisi, and finally to Poland, where his plane landed in a field that German aircraft had recently used. He returned to Poland a week before the Warsaw Uprising.

Novak's last trip from Warsaw to London was by train through Nazi Germany and then on foot across the border to neutral Switzerland, where he was arrested but eventually was allowed to leave for Britain. This trip from Poland to London took approximately one month.

Brezezinski rightly calls *Courier from Warsaw* "a gripping account of personal heroism." Nowak barely avoided arrest many times. To cite one instance: at the last moment Nowak decided not to attend a Resistance meeting in a Warsaw apartment house because he thought someone may have tipped off the Nazis. Just as he stepped out of the apartment house, a Nazi official in civilian clothes asked him what he was doing there. Nowak looked over his shoulder and saw a small brass plate with the name of a dentist. He said that he had just left the dentist. The Nazi official checked out his story by going to a nearby pharmacist and calling up the dentist. "Has a patient by the name of Jezorianski visited you?" he asked. (Jezorianski was Nowak's real name; he didn't take the name of Jan Nowak until a few months later.) The dentist said yes. Nowak writes: "The unknown woman, whom I had never seen and never would see, had not hesitated for a second. She understood in an instant that someone's life was at stake."

It is hard to convey how difficult daily life was in the Polish Underground. Novak had to memorize passwords, names, addresses, and the information he needed to pass on. He had to assume disguises (he often dressed up as a railway worker). He had to worry continually about informers. Many of Nowak's colleagues were arrested, tortured, and executed.

Novak was a successful courier insofar as he made it safely to London and gave the Polish government microfilmed documents as well as a great deal of information about the Home Army that he had memorized, but his conversations with British authorities left him frustrated and angry. They did not believe what he had to say about the extermination of Polish Jews.

St. Jude Children's®
Research Hospital

Finding cures. Saving children.
ALSAC · DANNY THOMAS, FOUNDER

stjude.org

When Novak returned to Poland a week before the Warsaw Uprising, he told the leaders of the Home Army that the Uprising "will not influence the policy of the Allies in the least." When ordinary Poles on the eve of the Warsaw Uprising asked him about Allied support, Nowak could not tell them what he really thought-- that the Allies were mainly concerned with pleasing Stalin. "I lied like a trooper. In this moment and mood, for all the money in the world I could not have brought myself to speak the truth."

The Chief of Staff of the Home Army agreed with Novak's grim assessment. "I have no illusions about what awaits us here after the Russians enter Warsaw and we come into the open," he said. "But even if the worst fate should befall me, I would prefer that to giving up without a fight. We must do our duty to the end."

Nowak and the leaders of the Home Army thought Prime Minister Mikolajczyk's trip to Moscow to negotiate with Stalin was pointless. Stalin made it clear that the government of post-war Poland would be chosen by him. He referred to the Polish Underground as "a handful of criminals." He accused the Home Army of beginning the Uprising too soon. A general in the Home Army told Nowak: "The Russians will accuse us whatever we do."

The Home Army, Nowak says, "waited in vain for relief by the Red Army, . . . [which] we could see plainly from my rooftop." Attempts by the Home Army to establish radio contact with the Red Army were unsuccessful.

Stalin wanted to destroy the Home Army because it was the army of the Polish government in London, which Stalin did not recognize. In *Inferno: The World at War: 1939-1945,* Max Hastings says the Soviet High Command issued the following order to Soviet commanders two weeks before the Uprising: "Soviet troops . . . have encountered Polish military detachments run by the Polish emigré government. These detachments have behaved suspiciously and have everywhere acted against the interests of the Red Army. Contact with them [is] therefore forbidden. When these formations are found, they must be immediately disarmed and sent to specially organised collection points for investigation."

After the Soviet takeover of Poland, members of the Resistance were arrested and sent to the Gulag.

Nowak's main function during the Uprising was to broadcast news to Britain—no other Resistance movement in Europe had an underground radio station— but the British press was mostly pro-Soviet and uninterested in Poland.

(In September 1944 George Orwell exploded: "I want to protest against the mean and cowardly attitude adopted by the British press towards the recent rising in Warsaw. ... One was left with the general impression that the Poles deserved to have their bottoms smacked for doing what all the Allied wirelesses had been urging them to do for years past.")

Nowak describes the death and devastation the Nazis wreaked on the Poles during the two months of the Uprising, but there is a glimmer of light in this dark chronicle. Nowak refers to a marriage that took place on the 37th day of the Uprising—his own. He told his girlfriend Greta, who was also in the Resistance: "The end is drawing near. Let's face it as husband and wife."

Nowak was a well-known figure in the Underground, so the chapel where they were married was filled though the Germans were only three hundred yards away. "We crunched up to the altar on broken glass—not one stained glass window in the chapel was unbroken. Our young priest was in a hurry. He had a funeral service scheduled next. The wedding ceremony took not more than seven minutes." After the ceremony Nowak and his wife went to the grave of his wife's sister, who had died a few days earlier. Returning to their quarters, Novak and his wife were given a surprise party. The owner of Warsaw's most famous delicatessen and grocery store provided a bottle of wine, a tin of meat, and two tins of sardines.

The Warsaw Uprising resulted in the deaths of 150,000 to 200,000 Polish civilians and 15,000 to 20,000 Resistance fighters. The Nazis made a systematic effort to raze the city and they forced its remaining occupants—now numbering about 700,000—to leave.

The Home Army General accepted full responsibility for the Warsaw Uprising. Novak did not think the General "regretted his decision or considered it to have been the wrong one. He maintained . . . that there was no alternative. To refrain from fighting the Germans at a moment when it was clear that they were in retreat would have been a departure from the line Poland had consistently followed since September 1939. . . . A massacre could have been avoided only by voluntarily giving way to Soviet puppets. If this had been done, in all probability the Red Army would have not stopped its advance at the edge of the city."

In December 1944 Novak and his wife left Poland—it was thought that if he travelled with his wife he would be less conspicuous—one month before Soviet troops crossed the Vistula River and took over Warsaw. After they arrived in London, Nowak gave a press conference in which he described the hell of the Uprising and called for "free elections guaranteed by the three powers and held under the supervision of British and American observers on the spot. They are the only way to save our future and the independence of Poland." Predictably, TASS, the official Soviet agency, called his statements "a pack of lies."

Nowak recalls his last conversation with Mikolajczyk, who continued to think that he could work out a deal with Stalin that would prevent the complete Soviet takeover of Poland. Nowak thought he was deluded. In a footnote Nowak says: "In March, 1945, the Soviets invited the leaders of Polish political parties. . . to a meeting to begin the negotiations to implement the Yalta agreement. All the guests were arrested, flown to Moscow, and put on trial."

The Warsaw Uprising, Nowak says, was based on an illusion. "Nothing could shake the Poles' deep-rooted faith that the western Allies would resist any open onslaught on the independence of Poland." Nowak and the leaders of the Home Army knew otherwise. "The fact remains that . . . neither the Soviet betrayal of the Warsaw Rising nor all that followed, including the arrest of a group of Polish leaders by the NKVD in 1945 and the rigged elections of 1947, would change by one iota the policy of the Western Allies."

Nowak calls the Uprising a "disaster," but he also thinks the Uprising helped Poles resist Soviet tyranny. In the Epilogue, which was written after the rise of Solidarity, Nowak says: "The Soviet betrayal of the Warsaw Rising left an invisible barrier between the Polish people and their communist rulers, an estrangement which subsequent communist governments never managed to overcome."

On the last page of the "Epilogue," Nowak remembers his bittersweet feelings about V-E Day in London. Britain had defeated the Nazis, but Poland now was occupied by Soviet troops. "Our day of victory will also come," he says.

In his review of *Courier* Jan Kott notes that in the early 1980s even though the Polish police seized and destroyed the printer's plates for the book "the second edition appeared soon thereafter. Like the first, it sold out immediately. . . . In Poland copies of Nowak's book are now passed surreptitiously from hand in hand."

After Poland became independent in 1989, Nowak returned to Poland frequently and he often appeared on Polish television. He moved to Warsaw in 2002, where he died in 2005.

Courier from Warsaw is a powerful memoir but in my view Novak's treatment of Churchill and the British government is harsher than is warranted. The British did help the Home Army; the Royal Air Force flew more than 200 sorties from bases in Britain and Italy to drop supplies and personnel in Poland. The majority of the pilots were Poles. The flights were dangerous and more than 30 aircraft were shot down.

The British continued to do airdrops during the Warsaw Uprising. Because Warsaw was burning, it was hard for pilots to see where Home Army forces were located, and many airdrops ended up in Nazi hands. Stalin claimed that 95% of the drops landed in Nazi-held territory, but this is an exaggeration. Until the final days of the Warsaw Uprising Stalin denied the Allies' request for the use of landing strips on Soviet-controlled territory. According to one report, the Soviets "even fired at Allied airplanes which carried supplies from

Italy and strayed into Soviet-controlled airspace."

Churchill wanted to do more to help the Home Army, but he did not have the support of Roosevelt, who thought Stalin must be placated. Roosevelt reportedly told a former U.S. ambassador to Moscow that he had a "hunch" that "if I give [Stalin] everything that I possibly can and ask nothing from him in return, noblesse oblige, he won't try to annex anything and will work for a world of democracy and peace."

Nowak knew otherwise, which is why he and his wife remained in London after the war. After working for the BBC for several years, he became head of the Polish Service of Radio Free Europe in 1952. In its obituary for Nowak the *Times* said: "He turned it into the main source of outside news for Poles under Communism." According to a report from RFE/RL, Pope John Paul II told Nowak that he used to listen to him while he shaved every morning. The *Times's* obituary also notes that Nowak was "an active campaigner for improved Polish-Jewish relations."

Reading *Courier from Warsaw*, I realized that Nowak had more near-death experiences in one morning than I had in a lifetime. Only twice in my life have I felt that I was near death. In Chapter One I mentioned the first incident: a car skidding out of control. The second time I was on a plane that was trying to land in strong winds at National Airport. The aircraft was shaking like a leaf as it approached the runway. Suddenly the aircraft jerked upwards and the captain said: "We executed a missed approach." The second time around we landed safely.

My wife has more in common with Nowak than I do because she experienced World War II first-hand. Born in 1940, she survived the siege of Budapest, when the Red Army was fighting retreating German troops and the remnants of the Hungarian Army. During the siege, which lasted from December 24 1944 to February 13 1945, 35,000 civilians died from the military operations or from starvation. My wife and her family survived by spending almost two months in the basement of their apartment building. Food was scarce. She remembers the excitement when her father and other men found a dead horse.

My wife read Nowak's book and so did her father. She wrote Nowak a letter of appreciation and he replied: "I am very happy to learn that you and your father liked Courier from Warsaw. The Hungarian-Polish friendship is so strong that it survived everything. In 1940 when you were born Hungarians offered tremendous help to Poles who tried to cross your country in order to reach the army in the west."

PART THREE:
AFTER WASHINGTON

CHAPTER 10

Part-Time Writer, Public Relations; Delivery Man, Printing Company

(Jobs #27 and #28)

In 1989 many people in the world celebrated the collapse of the Soviet Union and the birth of freedom in Eastern Europe. Jan Nowak could now visit Poland, which he had last seen in December 1944. I too was happy that Hungary, a country I had visited many times because my wife has relatives there, was now a free country whose citizens could travel anywhere. Yet I soon began to worry that the birth of freedom in Soviet bloc countries would eventually result in the death of my job.

I was right. Two years later Congress cut Radio Free Europe/Radio Liberty's budget by two/thirds. A year after the budget cut my job was abolished. I was unemployed again—the third time in two decades.

RFE/RL's Research Institute became part of George Soros's Open Society Institute. A few years later Soros decided not to fund it, but he kept the Research Institute's archives, which now belong to the Central European University. RFE/RL's Broadcasting Archives are housed at the Hoover Institution of Stanford University.

When I lost my job at Beaver College, I did not regret it because I disliked teaching. When I lost my job at RFE/RL I did regret it because I enjoyed writing the *Soviet/East European Report.* Many academics, journalists, and government officials told me they liked it. Robert Kaiser, who had been managing editor of the *Washington Post,* wrote: "I am a great fan of your Soviet East European Report."

It was a tough time. At the age of 53, when friends and relatives had high-level jobs in government, academia, medicine, or business, I was out of work. I did not tell Irving Kristol or Ben Wattenberg that I needed a job. It was too awkward to do so. Or maybe I was too proud.

I had been writing a newsletter for five years, so I thought I might be able to get a similar job, but I had to confine my job search to the Washington area because my wife had a good job with the Foreign Broadcast Information Service.

After applying for at least fifty jobs that required writing or editing, I got two interviews. One was for a half-time job as the book review editor of an influential quarterly; the other was for a full-time job as the editor of a quarterly dealing with academic affairs. I remember telling my 85-year-old mother, who was in the hospital, that there was a good chance I would get one of these jobs.

Two days later I learned that I didn't get the full-time job. That same day my mother died. A week later I learned that I didn't get the part-time job as book review editor.

Dickens's Micawber says something will turn up, but nothing turned up. In my self-pitying moments, which were rare, I said to myself I was a failure—a failed journalist, failed academic, failed bureaucrat, and now a failed neoconservative intellectual. In 1993 and 1994 I didn't publish a single essay or book review.

But I was not totally out of the neoconservative loop. I still had lunch with neocon friends and I occasionally attended a lecture at the American Enterprise Institute. I also belonged to a monthly discussion group on social and political issues held at the apartment of my friend Guenter Lewy, a retired professor of political science whom I had met when I was a fellow at AEI.

In *Death of a Salesman* Willy Loman's wife famously says "Attention must be paid." I preferred Mark Twain's remark: "Don't go around saying the world owes you a living. The world owes you nothing. It was here first." I thought of my father; he had always bounced back after being fired.

Was I resilient—to use a fashionable word—like my father? He could sell anything—from greeting cards to used cars. But my writing skills did not seem very marketable. I had never been a speechwriter or a ghost writer.

After a year something did turn up. I was hired by a major Washington public relations firm. It was not a full-time job; I would be paid by the hour. I met the head of the PR firm at his well-appointed office. He gave me two bottles of red wine from the vineyard he owned in Italy. He also gave me a trial assignment: write an op-ed about unnecessary government regulations for the head of a major corporation. He gave me some material to work with. I wrote what I thought was a good op-ed piece and sent it to him.

"Very good," he emailed me. "Now get it published in the *Wall Street Journal*."

I told him it was very hard to get an op-ed piece in the *Wall Street Journal* or any major newspaper.

"That's what I am paying you for," he said.

I did two more pieces for him that were rejected by several newspapers. Then he dropped me, but he did pay me for one month's work. My brief career in public relations was over, but the red wine he gave me was good.

I decided to quit looking for a job writing or editing. But what could I do? Although I disliked teaching, I applied to five area colleges for a job as a part-time adjunct professor of English. I didn't even get a response. I thought of applying for a job as a barista or a short-order cook but would a luncheonette or coffee shop hire a 54-year-old man with no experience? I ruled out manual labor— too old.

Then it occurred to me that I had one skill that was marketable: I could drive. I was about to apply for a job as a school bus driver when I saw a want-ad for a part-time driver for a printing company. I applied for it and got the job. It required me to pick up printed materials from a small printing company in Northern Virginia and deliver them to retail stores in suburban Maryland. The company gave me a small car to use. I was paid $35 a day for the work, which roughly took about four hours.

I liked this job because I like doing things fast—maneuvering in traffic, parking quickly, then running into a store and dropping off the printed materials. One time I parked in a handicapped spot. When I came out two cops were waiting for me.

"Do you know you parked in a handicapped space?" the taller one said.

"Sorry officer, I really didn't see it."

"You didn't see it? It's marked clear as day."

"Yes, officer," I said politely, "but you see it's my first week on this job delivering stuff and I just wasn't. . . ." I was lying. I knew it was a handicapped space but I figured it would only take me one minute to get back to the car. Moreover, it wasn't my first week on the job.

"Yeah, yeah, yeah," the cop said. Then he waved his hand. "Don't do it again."

"Thanks officer," I said.

Though I liked to do my job as quickly as possible, sometimes I talked to the owners of the stores that received my printing materials, which usually were invitations to weddings, Bar Mitzvahs. The stores I delivered print materials to mainly were greeting card stores or gift shops and almost all the owners were immigrants. How did I know? They spoke English with an accent. I remember talking to immigrants from Iran, Russia, Israel, and South Korea.

For many years I had been interested in immigrants and immigration policy. My grandparents were immigrants from Romania and Poland; my wife emigrated from Hungary in 1948. My wife and I have friends who emigrated from Germany, Poland, the Czech Republic, Slovakia, Slovenia, Iran, Ecuador, Mauritius, Hungary, and Great Britain. My primary care doctor is from India, my dermatologist is from Russia, my dentist is from Venezuela. Our older daughter is married to a South African immigrant (ethnically Greek). The woman who cuts my hair is from Vietnam.

In 2013 I published an article about Henry James and immigration. In *The American Scene* (1907), a book about his impressions of America after a two decade absence, James wrote about the new immigrants to America, who mainly were Italians and East European Jews. James thought the new Italian immigrants were not as charming as the Italians he met in Italy and he also thought that the new Jewish immigrants were mangling the English language, but he was certain that the new immigrants would be assimilated. "The machinery of assimilation," he says, "is colossal."

My essay on James became part of a book I wrote called *Walking New York: Reflections of American Writers from Walt Whitman to Teju Cole* (2014). I argued that James was right—that the new immigrants did assimilate. I also argued that New York's run-down and crime-ridden neighborhoods were restored mainly by immigrants who ran small businesses. A recent book on New York makes a similar point. Since 1978 New York has become home to more than 1.5 million immigrants from all over the world; they have transformed the city. They are "half the city's accountants and nurses, 40 percent of its doctors, real estate brokers and property managers."

In March 2021 Fareed Zakaria, an immigrant from India, wrote: "With pandemic restrictions on top of everything else, immigration to the United States has plunged to levels not seen in four decades. Some of the world's best and brightest are choosing to go to more hospitable countries, from Canada to Australia. Census data show that without immigration, the United States faces a dire demographic future. It would mean fewer people and especially fewer young people, which would mean less growth, dynamism and opportunity for everyone."

In 2021 there were many articles about a female scientist who emigrated from Hungary to the United States in 1985: Kati Kariko. In April 2021 the *New York Times* called her "one of the heroes of

Covid-19 vaccine development. Her work, with her close collaborator Dr. Drew Weissmann of the University of Pennsylvania, laid the foundation for the stunningly successful vaccines made by Pfizer-BioNTech and Moderna."

WALTER LAQUEUR

One of the most prominent immigrants I met was Walter Laqueur, who wrote many books on twentieth-century history as well as books about anti-Semitism, Zionism, and terrorism. Laqueur was a friend of my friend Guenter Lewy. Both Laqueur and Lewy came from Breslau and both left Nazi Germany in the late 1930s—emigrating to Palestine. Lewy came to the U.S. in the late 1940s, where he got a Ph.D. from Columbia University. Laqueur, who briefly attended Hebrew University in Jerusalem, lived in Palestine/Israel for fifteen years. He moved to London in 1955. A decade later he began to spend half the year in Washington and half in London. In *Jews and Germans: Promise, Tragedy, and the Search for Normalcy* (2020), Lewy says Laqueur was one of many Jewish immigrants from Nazi Germany who "achieved prominence."

In his autobiography, *Thursday's Child Has Far to Go: A Memoir of the Journeying Years* (1992), Laqueur says that Lewy became a successful academic, specializing in the history of political thought. In *Generation Exodus: The Fate of Young Jewish Refugees from Nazi Germany* (2004), Laqueur mentions another emigre from Breslau: Abraham Ascher, also a successful academic (a historian of Russia). Ascher, who also became a friend, was my boss at the National Endowment for the Humanities.

Laqueur, who died in 2018, was never a friend of mine. I knew him because I met him at least a half-dozen times at dinner parties at the apartment of Lewy and his wife Ilse. The first two or three times we met he struck me as somewhat aloof, as if he were bored with the conversation, but I always found what he had to say about twentieth-century history interesting. When he remarried after his wife died in 1995 he became more sociable—more interested in what other people had to say. I remember him asking my wife about her childhood in wartime Budapest.

Laqueur, like Jan Nowak, wrote about the British government's lack of interest in the mass murder of Jews. In *The Terrible Secret: Suppression of the Truth about Hitler's 'Final Solution,'* (1980) Laqueur cites the Polish edition of *Courier from Warsaw*, saying that "Nowak fully confirms certain aspects of Jan Karski's evidence [about the mass murder of Jews], especially with regard to the reception in London. He [Nowak] was the first emissary to arrive from Poland after the battle of the Warsaw Ghetto. . . . He dwelt at length on the fate of the Jews but there was no interest whatsoever in this topic, with the exception of one counter-intelligence officer who was personally deeply moved."

In the English-language version of *Courier from Warsaw*, published two years after *The Terrible Secret,* Nowak says, "Walter Laqueur refers to my role as an emissary who brought information and documents about the ghetto rising and the Holocaust to London."

Laqueur, who was twelve when the Nazis came to power, says he was not harassed or beaten up by non-Jewish schoolmates, but he slowly came to realize that the Nazis would remain in power and therefore there was no future for Jews in Germany. In July 1938 he witnessed a Gymnastics and Athletics Festival at which Hitler, Himmler, and Goebbels spoke. "The mass enthusiasm was genuine and impressive. Those in attendance certainly believed in Hitler and Nazism; many faces radiated belief in the Führer."

On November 7 1938, at the age of 17, Laqueur left Germany, taking a train to Trieste, from where he went by ship to Palestine. He left two days before Kristallnacht. His parents, whom he never saw again, died four years later in Auschwitz.

"The world I had known as a boy no longer existed," Laqueur says in his memoir, "and as I tried to remember the people I had known when I was 16, I realized that most of them had died a violent death."

The dead included non-Jewish school friends who were killed "in the ruins of Stalingrad," but most of the dead were Jews.

Laqueur knew of one Jew—he only mentions his last name (Blumenfeld) —who remained in Germany and survived. After escaping from a concentration camp "a woman hid him in her cellar for two years, until the day the Russians arrived." I know two Jews—one from Poland, another from Slovakia—who escaped death because they were hidden by non-Jews for two years. In the latter case a farmer hid a family of four in an attic.

Laqueur tried to persuade a Jewish girlfriend to emigrate, but her mother was in poor health so she did not want to leave. She died in Auschwitz. In the late 1930s it was extremely difficult for German Jews to emigrate even if they wanted to. Jews spent hours at consulates looking for jobs in a foreign country. "The scenes in these offices were the most harrowing that I can remember. No one was shouting or weeping; there was only deep, unrelieved gloom." After the outbreak of World War II in September 1939 "it became exceedingly difficult to leave the country," Laqueur writes in *Generation Exodus*. Yet he notes that even in 1941, some eight thousand Jews left Germany before October, "when Himmler gave the order to stop emigration altogether."

It was also difficult to emigrate to Palestine, which was under a British mandatory government. "After 1936, immigration to Palestine became restricted," Laqueur says in *Generation Exodus*. "Only a limited number of immigration certificates were issued for workers and there was an ever- lengthening waiting list." In 1939 the British curtailed immigration even further. Laqueur got a certificate of emigration because he had been accepted as a student at Hebrew University in Jerusalem. When he was living in Palestine he tried in vain to get certificates for his parents. "They did not belong to any of the few categories that still qualified, and they were too old for illegal immigration."

In 1946, when Laqueur was a reporter for a Jerusalem newspaper, he watched as British authorities refused to let Jewish refugees disembark at Haifa. (The refugees were sent to detention camps in Cyprus.)

The scene moved him deeply, and he broke down. "Some chord had been struck; the whole tragedy of my family, of so many friends and acquaintances, of European Jewry . . . became alive as a result of this chance encounter."

Laqueur, like Nowak, viewed the end of World War II with mixed emotions. "I remember that I did not feel much joy that day. . . . I felt more like mourning and my heart was full of doubts and forebodings. Long ago I had given up hope of ever seeing my parents and the other members of my family again. But it was one thing to suspect the worst and another to have final certainty."

Laqueur did not feel much joy that day for another reason; he thought a war between Arabs and Jews was inevitable. He was glad when the U.N. voted for partitioning Palestine in November 1947, but he was "not among those dancing in the streets."

When war broke out in December 1947 Laqueur, his wife, and their six-week-old baby were living in an Arab village near Jerusalem. They had to move, but the apartment they found in Jerusalem was exposed to sniper fire from Arabs on a hill a few hundred yards away. A few months later, after the neighborhood was heavily shelled, Laqueur decided to move his family again—this time to a small hotel in the center of Jerusalem.

Jerusalem was one of the most dangerous places for Jews to be during this war because "there were relatively few young people, and of these a fairly high percentage were physically or mentally unfit to carry arms." When the Arabs blocked all roads to Jerusalem, food and water were rationed. The siege was lifted in mid-April, but the war for Jerusalem lasted until July.

The death toll in Jerusalem during the seven-month war was much lower than the death toll for the Warsaw Ghetto Uprising in 1943 or the Warsaw general uprising in 1944. Seven hundred Israeli civilians died and 600 Israeli soldiers. (The number of Arab deaths is unknown.) Nevertheless, living in Jerusalem at the time was very dangerous, since sniper fire was commonplace. Laqueur lost several friends and acquaintances. Laqueur himself barely escaped death while walking in the city. Sixty feet in front of him a young boy in uniform was instantly killed by an explosion.

The war of Independence, Laqueur writes in *Generation Exodus,* "was the bloodiest by far of all the Israeli wars." On April 22 1948 Laqueur wrote: "I cannot continue my diary tonight. There is no electricity. No one is surprised or angry. No one is asking why. This is Jerusalem, the capital, at the end of April, 1948, total chaos prevails, *tohuvabohu* (Genesis 1:2)." *Tohuvabohu* is the Hebrew word for chaos. This excerpt from his diary was published on May 6—eight days before Ben-Gurion proclaimed the new state of Israel.

Laqueur's description of his life in Jerusalem during the seven-month war is riveting, but in my view the most powerful chapter in his memoir is the first one, which is about his return to Breslau approximately twenty-five years after he left it. Sixty percent of Breslau had been destroyed in the war, but what struck Laqueur the most was Breslau's transformation. It was no longer a German city; it was now a city in Poland called Wroclaw. In 1945 the Allies had moved Poland's boundaries westward.

When Laqueur was growing up, he never met a single Pole. Now everyone on the streets and in the shops in Wroclaw was speaking Polish. "There was not a single soul known to me, and all the names of streets and shops and people had changed."

On the last page of his memoir Laqueur says: "I wrote this account of the first part of my life because I lived through a period of history full of drama and tragedy, an era which is now receding into the distant past. . . . Many of my contemporaries did not survive, and in this respect, as in some others, I was lucky." Jan Nowak would probably make the same statement about himself and his contemporaries.

One reads the memoirs of Nowak and Laqueur with wonder and admiration: how were they able to write about death and destruction with lucidity and detachment? They are not unique in their ability to write about twentieth-century horrors. Many writers who were imprisoned by Hitler, Stalin, Mao, Pol Pot, and Castro have written powerful accounts of their experiences.

I recently read *One Hundred Miracles: A Memoir of Music and Survival,* by the Czech harpsichordist Zuzana Ružičková, who was Jewish. The Nazis deported her first to Terezin and then to Auschwitz, then to a forced labor group in Hamburg, and finally to Bergen-Belsen. Living in unspeakable conditions, she often thought of Bach—or even played Bach in her mind. "Bach has sustained me through every trial of my life and remained with me as a comfort in old age. I owe him my life."

It would be absurd to say that I have anything in common with Laqueur. I have led a sheltered life, a life without fear. Secondly, my working life has nothing in common with Laqueur's. He is a major historian who wrote many highly regarded books. He also held many important jobs; he was the Editor-in-Chief of the *Holocaust Encyclopedia,* the Director of the Institute of Contemporary History in London, and the Chairman of the Inernational Research Council of the Center for Strategic and International Studies in Washington.

Yet we do have a few minor things in common. We both grew up in secular Jewish households; we both took up many sports when we were teens; we both skipped a grade and for much of our lives were younger than our colleagues; and we both worked at many jobs. Laqueur's jobs were more exotic than mine. In Germany he worked in a textile factory. In Palestine he worked as an agricultural laborer on a kibbutz; he also worked as an armed guard for a kibbutz, riding a horse.

Laqueur never liked manual labor, but he says his jobs in a factory and on a kibbutz were "an important part of my education, even if I did not appreciate it at the time. It certainly broadened my horizon and improved my judgment. But for this experience I would probably have gone on reasoning on all kinds of important issues on a theoretical level, probably expressing all kinds of extreme views, as I did at seventeen." A few lines later he asks: "What do they know who spend their whole life in an academic community or similar sheltered surroundings?"

When Laqueur wrote these remarks, he may have been thinking of left-wing academics whose blueprints for political and economic change were not grounded in reality. I have no animus against academia—I have many academic friends—yet I am happy that I did not get tenure at Beaver College and happy that I did not get another academic job. If I had spent my life teaching English I would never have met the people who in various ways enriched my life.

Sometimes I drive past an exit sign on I-287 in Northern New Jersey that says Ramapo College of New Jersey. In 1974, as I said in an earlier chapter, I was interviewed twice for a job teaching English at Ramapo, but at the last moment a student told the faculty hiring committee that I was a fascist. If I had been hired at Ramapo I never would have worked in Washington. When I drive past that exit sign I often say to my wife: "Thank God that woman denounced me!"

CHAPTER 11

Househusband/Freelance Writer

(Job #29)

My job delivering printed materials was not difficult but the job's benefits—$35/day—were paltry and the job's costs were high. I had no time to attend lectures in Washington, no time to have lunch with friends, and very little time to write. So after six months I quit.

What did my wife think? I remembered a song Peggy Lee sang entitled "Why Don't You Do Right Like Some Other Men Do?" It's about a woman who complains that her man sponges off her. But my wife didn't complain. She was—to use a trite word—supportive. She knew that for a year I had looked in vain for a job. She knew that spending four to five hours a day making $35 made no sense. And she knew we wouldn't starve because she had a good job with the Foreign Broadcast Information Service.

I made my wife an offer she did not refuse. I would become a househusband—doing most of the shopping, cooking, and cleaning. We had already split the cooking and shopping. Now I would do about 90% of it. She would cook for parties and special occasions. The shopping and cooking worked out fine but not the cleaning. I didn't get good marks as a cleaner, and eventually we hired a house-cleaning service. Our financial situation improved slightly because I turned 55 and I could draw on an annuity from RFE/RL, which amounted to about $1000/month.

So at the age of 55 I had three ways of defining myself. I could call myself a retiree, which is how I described myself on credit card applications. I could call myself a househusband or homemaker, but I never did. Or I could call myself a freelance writer, which I usually did, though I thought it was disingenuous to imply that I made a living by writing, since I usually made no more than $2000 a year.

If someone at a dinner party said to me: "What do you do?" I sometimes would jokingly respond by saying "Not a damn thing." Or: "I play tennis and make soups." When the questioner looked puzzled, I said I was a freelance writer,

"So what do you write?" I was often asked.

"Non-fiction."

"What kind of non-fiction?"

"History—mainly eighteenth-century intellectual history."

That usually ended the conversation unless the person asking me the question was a big reader.

Since I could never make a living as a writer, why did I still want to write? Why didn't I take up gardening or playing chess or bird-watching or furniture-making or learning to play the clarinet, an instrument I've always loved? The thought of giving up writing never crossed my mind. Why would I stop doing something I enjoyed—something I was moderately successful at?

Writers often talk about the agony of writing. George Orwell said that "writing a book is a horrible, exhausting struggle, like a long bout of some painful illness." It makes no sense to compare writing a book to having a painful illness. I cannot imagine spending many hours doing something one finds painful when the end result is so uncertain. I've failed to find publishers for three books I've written, but I don't think I wasted my time writing these books. I enjoyed the research and enjoyed the writing. I also managed to publish several articles based on material in these books.

In "Why I Write" Orwell gives four reasons that motivate people to write: sheer egotism, aesthetic enthusiasm, historical purpose, and political purpose. By sheer egotism Orwell means "the desire to seem clever, to be talked about, to be remembered after death, to get your own back on grown-ups who snubbed you in childhood, etc. etc." I don't think sheer egotism was a strong motivating force for me. Aesthetic enthusiasm has been a stronger motivating force—or, as Orwell puts it, the pleasure one gets out of "words and their right arrangement."

Sidney Hook offers a different motive for writing: "the excitement of clarifying ideas." I agree. When I begin to write about a subject my ideas are blurry. It is as if I'm looking through binoculars and everything is out of focus. By writing I slowly get a subject in focus. I slowly clarify my thoughts and organize them—I hope—into a coherent narrative.

To my mind writing is like playing tennis. You have to enjoy playing regardless of the outcome. I enjoy playing a guy who beats me nineteen times out of twenty. Yet I wonder: Would I have continued to enjoy writing if editors had rejected 19 out of 20 things I had written?

There is a curse that goes: "May you get everything you wish for." Losing my job and not finding another full-time job was—deep down—something I had wished for. (I did not tell my wife that.) I now had plenty of time to write. I felt reasonably confident that I would have some success as a writer, by which I mean I would get published. I never thought I would make a lot of money writing.

The first question I asked myself in 1996 was: What should I write? I ruled out trying to write something that might be popular. I knew I could not write a self-help book about how to achieve serenity, happiness, longevity etc. I didn't have a difficult childhood, so I couldn't write a memoir about being beaten, neglected, sexually abused, or mentally stifled. I never was a drug addict or alcoholic. I had not served in the military or climbed Mount Everest.

You get the point: I had no dramatic stories to tell. The worst thing that happened to me as a child was a bad compound fracture of my left arm, which put me in the hospital for two weeks when I was nine years old.

I also ruled out writing fiction, which I had tried two decades earlier. And I ruled out writing about foreign policy or Eastern Europe. I had done that for the past decade. I mainly wanted to write about eighteenth-century English literature—my favorite literary period. So I wrote essays about David Hume, Edmund Burke, and Samuel Johnson.

The essay about Burke appeared in the *Partisan Review*, a magazine I had some connection with since the mid-1960s, when I took a course with its editor, William Phillips, who died in 2002. I wrote five essays for *Partisan Review,* but only one essay was about an eighteenth-century writer. The others were about materialism, which I defended; Michel Foucault, whom I attacked; Henry Adams, whom I also attacked; and Radio Free Europe, which I praised.

The article on Samuel Johnson appeared in the *Sewanee Review*. It was reprinted in *The New Rambler,* a magazine published by the Johnson Society of London, so I passed muster with Johnson scholars! I was happy to appear in the *Sewanee Review,* which published many writers I admired, including Cleanth Brooks, whose course on Romantic poetry I had taken at Yale. George Core, the magazine's editor, also reconnected me with my Rutgers grad school mentor John McCormick. I reviewed a collection of McCormick's essays for the magazine.

Sewanee Review published three essays of mine on eighteenth-century writers—Samuel Johnson, Edward Gibbon, and Joseph Addison—plus one on Orwell as well as two autobiographical essays: "God and Bugs Bunny" and "Memoirs of a New York Intellectual Manqué." When Core retired in 2016 after serving 43 years as editor, I stopped sending essays to the *Sewanee Review* because I assumed—maybe wrongly— that the new editor would not be interested in my writing.

The essay of mine that got the most attention, "A Note on the Banality of Evil," appeared in the *Wilson Quarterly* in 1998. The magazine's editor told me he received more mail about this essay than anything he had ever published. The banality of evil is a phrase Hannah Arendt used to describe Adolf Eichmann in *Eichmann in Jerusalem: A Report on the Banality of Evil* (1963). I argued that the phrase, which still is popular, is meaningless. "Banal is an aesthetic term, not a moral one. It applies more to ideas . . . . Evil acts . . . are neither banal nor not banal. The term banality does not apply to evil, just as it does not apply to goodness."

Arendt said she wasn't referring to what Eichmann did. She was referring to his character; he was a banal bureaucrat obeying Hitler's orders— a thoughtless man who "has no motives at all." Yet she also said Eichmann was a fanatical worshiper of Hitler. "Eichmann's fanatical devotion to Hitler," I wrote, "led him to rejet Heinrich Himmler's order in the last year of the war to stop the Final Solution." In the last year of the war Eichmann rounded up more than 600,000 Hungarian Jews and sent them to Auschwitz.

Six years after my essay appeared, David Cesarani, an English historian, published a biography of Eichmann (*Becoming Eichmann*), in which he questioned Arendt's characterization of Eichmann. "Eichmann was a forceful personality who acted with zeal and initiative," Cesarani says. Reviewing *Becoming Eichmann*, Ian Kershaw, a leading British historian of the Nazi era, wrote that "a central purpose of Cesarani's penetrating and compelling study is to show how wrong Arendt's influential interpretation of Eichmann was, and how misleading the phrase 'banality of evil' has proved."

After writing about the banality of evil, I went back to writing about the Enlightenment. In 2001 I published *Three Deaths and Enlightenment Thought: Hume, Johnson, and Marat,* in which I argued that many Enlightenment writers and painters were preoccupied with how people died. I also argued that it was misguided to call the

Enlightenment The Age of Reason. The major Enlightenment writers thought man was driven by "the perplexity of contending passions," to quote Samuel Johnson. Hume and Johnson disagreed about the effect that religion has on the passions, but they both agreed that economic growth promotes moderate passions—reducing the likelihood of violent civil discord.

Immersing myself in eighteenth-century British culture, I noticed that many writers—Addison, Fielding, Swift, Hume, and Johnson—wrote about conversation. They would agree with Hume, who said: "What can be expected from Men who never consulted Experience in any of their Reasonings, or who never search'd for that Experience, where alone it is to be found, in common Life and Conversation?" With roughly 500 coffeehouses and innumerable clubs, eighteenth-century London was a city of conversation. William Hogarth, however, implied that in most clubs there was too much drinking to have good conversation. In "Modern Midnight Conversation," one of Hogarth's most popular prints, the men are so drunk that they are incapable of having a conversation. There are twenty-three empty wine bottles in the room.

In 2006 I published *Conversation: A History of a Declining Art*, which includes many quotations from eighteenth-century British writers on the art of conversation. I noted that "in Fanny Burney's novel *Evelina* (1778), the first thing she says about Lord Orville, the man she will eventually marry, is: 'His conversation was sensible and spirited.'"

The reception of *Conversation*, published by Yale University Press, was much better than I had expected. (A blurb from Harold Bloom, the most well-known American literary critic, certainly helped make the book a success.) *Conversation* got the lead review in the *New York Review of Books* and the (London) *Times Literary Supplement*. There were reviews—almost all favorable—in newspapers and magazines in the United States, Britain, India, and Australia. The *New York Times's* cultural critic wrote a column about the book. I appeared on CBS-TV's "Sunday Morning" and on numerous radio talk shows in the United States, Britain, and Australia. The book was translated into Korean and Turkish.

The most interesting radio interview was with Diane Riehm, whose show had many listeners throughout the U.S. The show included an hour of questions from listeners. My favorite was from a Brit who said he was driving across the U.S. with some mates. He agreed with my comment that raillery and banter are essential ingredients for good conversation. He also said that after playing rugby he and his mates go out for a pint and have great conversations. In my book I write about the good conversations I had with my tennis buddies after we finished playing.

I made more money from *Conversation* than from anything I had ever written, but I'm talking about $10,000, not $100,000. I did get a trip to Melbourne, all expenses paid, to talk at the Melbourne Literary Festival. Robert Dessaix, a leading Australian essayist, liked my book and recommended me to the people running the festival. The festival organizers asked me to teach a one-day seminar on how to write non-fiction, which I did. I also was on a panel about non-fiction writing.

The highlight of the festival—for me—was being interviewed by Dessaix on the art of conversation. I remember walking up to the theater where I would be interviewed and seeing a long line of people waiting to get in. They were waiting to hear me—the guru of conversation! The theater soon was packed. When the interview was over, there was a long round of applause.

My wife and I had a great week in Melbourne, a lively city with good food and good coffeehouses. The hotel we were staying at had an awesome breakfast buffet. At the buffet I remember talking to Thomas Keneally, a leading Australian writer, and also to Alec Waugh, a genial man who is the grandson of Evelyn Waugh.

After a week in Melbourne, we spent a week in Sydney— more spectacular in its setting than Melbourne. I was asked to talk at a literary festival in Brisbane but—foolishly—I turned it down.

Conversation was so successful that I had no trouble getting a publisher for my next book. Harvard University Press gave me a

$5000 advance for *The Peculiar Life of Sundays,* a book on the history of Sabbath observance. Why did I want to write a book on Sabbath observance? I have no idea.

This book got mostly good reviews and it also got me another appearance on CBS-TV's "Sunday Morning" but it was a commercial failure. Harvard never recouped the advance it gave me.

I could not find a publisher for my next book, which was about Joseph Addison, who with Richard Steele founded the *Spectator,* a journal that in book form was the most widely read publication in England and colonial America. But I published three articles on Addison. The *Times Literary Supplement* published my article on Addison's *Cato,* which was George Washington's favorite play and the most popular eighteenth-century English play. In "The Strange Career of Joseph Addison," which appeared in the *Sewanee Review,* I talked about the dramatic decline in Addison's reputation in the twentieth century. In the eighteenth century he was admired by most of the major writers, including Hume and Johnson, but in the twentieth century he was dismissed as smug and superficial. Walter Jackson Bate, a leading Johnson scholar, wrote that Addison "gratified the fashionable tea-table morality of the day." This was not Samuel Johnson's view of Addison. Addison, he said, "knew the heart of man, from the depths of stratagem to the surface of affectation."

In April 2017 I published an article in the *Wall Street Journal* about Addison's importance—noting that, as one scholar puts it, he "was regarded for many generations as one of the most significant English writers of his time." Writing under the persona of Mr. Spectator (as did his collaborator Richard Steele), Addison talked about the pleasures of walking in London. In one essay, he praises the Royal Exchange, a two-level structure, built in 1669 around a great courtyard, that housed shops and boutiques. The Exchange, Addison said, made "this Metropolis a kind of Emporium for the Whole earth."

Addison implies that the many immigrants he met there had helped transform London into a bustling commercial center. "Sometimes I am jostled among a Body of Armenians; sometimes I am lost in a

Crowd of Jews; and sometimes make one in a Groupe of Dutch-men. I am a Dane, Swede or French-Man at different times." He was "wonderfully delighted to see such a Body of Men thriving in their own private Fortunes, and at the same time promoting the Publick Stock." Addison was saying what Adam Smith would say 65 years later: the self-interested pursuit of profit in most cases benefits the nation as a whole.

I did get a publisher for my next book: *Walking New York: Reflections of American Writers from Walt Whitman to Teju Cole* (2014). This book, which was published by Fordham University Press, was mentioned in the *New York Times* and it was favorably reviewed in the *Times Literary Supplement* and the *Wall Street Journal*. Moreover, the *New York Observer* called it one of the ten best books of the fall of 2014.

So my life as a freelance writer has been up and down. Though I failed to find a publisher for my next book, which was about writers and war, I published many articles on a variety of subjects in the *Weekly Standard* and the *Wall Street Journal*. Several were about eighteenth-century writers I admired. In November 2018 I published a piece about Bernard Mandeville, a precursor of Adam Smith.

Little is known about Mandeville, whom Benjamin Franklin called "a most facetious, entertaining companion." His main work is *The Fable of the Bees: or, Private Vices, Publick Benefits*, published in 1714. This work influenced Hume, Voltaire and Samuel Johnson. In the twentieth century the political economist Friedrich Hayek called Mandeville a "mastermind."

The private vices Mandeville praises are envy, ambition and avarice. His analysis of envy is especially interesting. Though Mandeville admits envy can be a destructive force, he argues that some people transform envious feelings into emulation, which promotes industriousness. Emulative envy, Mandeville contends, cannot flourish in traditional societies, since there are few opportunities for the poor to emulate the rich. Summarizing Mandeville's view, E. J. Hundert says that in modern predominantly commercial societies envy could be "directed into politically harmless and socially beneficial channels."

In April 2019 I published "Envy—the good kind," in *The New Criterion*. I noted that Hesiod in *Works and Days* speaks of two kinds of envy—the destructive kind and the emulative kind. In his entry for envy in the *Philosophical Dictionary,* Voltaire mentions Hesiod's praise of envy and then says: "I think Mandeville . . . is the first writer [since Hesiod] who tried to prove that envy is a very good thing, a very useful passion." Voltaire addresses the question of whether emulation is a type of envy. "Perhaps we can say that emulation is a type of envy—the only type of envy that keeps itself within the bounds of decency."

I like to think—perhaps I'm deluding myself— that I have been driven by emulative envy rather than destructive envy. I have learned how to write essays by emulating other essayists—including Joseph Addison, Samuel Johnson, William Hazlitt, George Orwell, and in our own day Joseph Epstein. I don't think I have been driven by the destructive kind of envy, though undoubtedly I get some pleasure when reading a negative review of a work by a writer I think is overrated.

CHAPTER 12

Semi-Househusband/ Freelance Writer

(Job #29A)

Why do I speak of Job #29A? Because this job, if we can call it a job, differs only slightly from my previous job. After my wife retired in 2010 I did less shopping though I still did most of the cooking. (My wife did most of the babysitting and driving for the two of our three grandsons who live nearby.) So I no longer was a full-time househusband. I had more time to write, and I began researching a book on writers and war. I read many books about World War I and many books about Vietnam.

My book on writers and war failed to find a publisher, but my research on this topic resulted in one of my best essays: "The Other McCarthy," which appeared in the *New Criterion* in June 1916. It's about the quarrel between Brigadier General Robbie Risner, who was a POW in North Vietnam, and Mary McCarthy, who in *Hanoi* (1968) wrote about meeting Risner. In *Hanoi* (1968) and in a subsequent article in the *New York Review of Books* (March 7, 1974) she implied that Risner was stupid, servile, and duplicitous.

I strongly disagreed with McCarthy's characterization of General Risner. Several leading journalists, including Anthony Lewis and James Fallows, also disagreed with McCarthy's portrait of General

Risner. So did Frances Kiernan, McCarthy's biographer. In *Seeing Mary Plain, A Life of Mary McCarthy* (2000), Kiernan says: "She went out of her way to attack him."

Born in Mammoth Spring, Arkansas, James Robinson Risner— known as Robbie Risner— grew up in Tulsa, Oklahoma. In *The Passing of the Night: My Seven Years as a Prisoner of the North Vietnamese* (1973), Risner writes about his hardscrabble childhood. "During those early years Dad had a small stockyard and had just purchased several thousand hogs when the stock market crashed. Broke and poor as church mice, we moved to Pumpkin Center, Oklahoma, where we lived on oil-leased land while Dad traded horses and cattle. ... Every night we went to sleep with the smell of gas and the sounds of oil-well engines and the shackle rods running back and forth."

In high school Risner worked at odd jobs. He was a stock clerk, a welder, and a rodeo rider. When his father went into the used car business, he washed and waxed his cars. He liked to ride motorcycles and tame wild horses. "My father told me I had a special knack with horses."

It was Risner's ambition to be a fighter pilot. In 1942, when he was eighteen, he enlisted in the Air Force Cadets. After two years of flight training, he flew P-38 and P-39 fighters but he never saw combat. After the war he joined the Oklahoma National Guard, which was called up when the Korean War began but was not sent to Korea. Risner was disappointed, so he left the Guard and signed up as a reconnaissance pilot in Korea. After flying ten missions, he persuaded the Air Force to let him become a fighter pilot. He soon became one of the best American airmen. He flew 109 combat missions in an F-86, shooting down eight MIG-15s.

When the Korean War ended, Risner—now a major—remained in the Air Force, continuing to fly F-86s. In 1957 he was chosen to commemorate the thirtieth anniversary of Charles Lindbergh's nonstop flight across the Atlantic. Refueling in the air twice, Risner flew an F-100F, a two-seat trainer aircraft, from Brooklyn to Paris in six hours, thirty-seven minutes. Lindbergh's flight had taken thirty-three hours, thirty minutes.

In 1964 Risner began flying combat missions in Vietnam. On March 16 1965 he was shot down for the first time—hit by ground fire while attacking a radar site in North Vietnam. He flew to the Tonkin Gulf, where he ejected safely. "For some unknown reason," Risner writes, "this mission was written up in *Time* magazine [April 23, 1965] with my picture on the cover. At the time it was a great honor. But later, in prison, I would have much cause to regret that *Time* had ever heard of me." The North Vietnamese "had a distorted view of my own importance in America. . . . They felt the *Time* article made me unique."

In August 1965 Risner flew a mission a day over North Vietnam. On September 16, 1965, Risner's luck ran out. Hit by ground fire, he tried to fly to the ocean, but his engine quit before he got there, and he bailed out. He was captured by local militia. He did not think he would be a POW for very long because he was told that Defense Secretary Robert McNamara had said the war would be over by June 1966. When a fellow POW said: "Hey, Robbie, just remember, the first year is the hardest," Risner wanted to slug him. "I could not bear the thought of being there a whole year."

Risner was a POW for seven years, four months, and twenty-seven days. When he was released, he said: "I'm awfully glad I didn't know . . . what was ahead of me. In my wildest imagination I had no idea American prisoners of war would be treated as inhumanely and cruelly as we were."

In *The Passing of the Night* Risner describes the first cell he was put in. "I felt as if someone had put me in a clothes closet. . . . I already hated that stinking small cell. Long flying cockroaches were everywhere. Rats were running back and forth at random under the door and through the drain hole at the bottom of the wall. The mice were profuse and spiders were all over. Since I had failed to put up my mosquito net the night before, the insects nearly carried me off. My feet looked like pincushions."

Soon Risner was moved from this cell to one in The Zoo, a prison about five miles from the so-called Hanoi Hilton, where most POWs were kept. It was not as small as the first cell, but it had no bunk and no place to hang a mosquito net. Two years later, when he was moved to a cell in the Hanoi Hilton, Risner heard a clatter outside the cell's window. "I realized that my only source of light was being closed off." The North Vietnamese were punishing him for being a defiant POW. "Despite the fact that they had really hurt me badly, they evidently did not feel that I was coming through for them enough."

Locked in a totally dark cell, Risner became agitated. "Absolute panic had set in. . . . Sheer desolation permeated that miserable dark cell that I lived in twenty-four hours a day. I was absolutely convinced that I would never get to leave that cell until the war was over. . . . I was not scared of anything that they would put me through because I felt that they had already done their worst. But I was terrified because I could not get rid of the panic."

Reviewing *The Passing of the Night,* Anthony Lewis wrote that Risner's "description of his terror while alone is by far the most impressive part of his book."

Risner speaks of "the torture programs" that were used "to get confessions to being a criminal. To my knowledge they got one from everyone in the camp. They printed them in the *Vietnam Courier,* and they forced some guys to read them on the radio." Though Risner felt terrible about signing a statement that he was a war criminal, he knew there were limits to a person's resistance. He sent out a directive to the POWs. "Resist until you are tortured, but do not take torture to the point where you lose your capability to think and do not take torture to the point where you lose the permanent use of your limbs." When two POWs felt terrible about signing anti-war statements after being tortured, a POW in a neighboring cell relayed a message from Risner: "We have all broken. Now blow smoke up their ass."

In an April 2000 interview, Risner said: "We maintained that we were never broken, that we were bent badly but never broken." Risner was eventually awarded a Second Air Force Cross for courage under torture and for "establishing an honorable standard that could be followed by others."

In the 1970s living conditions improved slightly for most POWs, though less so for the defiant ones like Risner. All the POWs had to cope with boredom. "The distinctive character of imprisonment in a North Vietnamese prison camp," Risner writes, "was the suffocating monotony . . . the pervasive sameness of the routine, over and over, day and out. Bodies built for movement were confined to closet-like boxes."

Prayer helped many POWs cope with boredom and despair. Risner prayed before he ate, which he had always done, prayed while being tortured, prayed when he was chained to his bed and could not exercise, prayed when he felt he was going out of his mind. "When the pressure started to build up, I would pray. I would explain my problems . . . and ask God for strength to make it." Risner says he "could not have existed if I had not been able to pray."

Risner not only prayed for himself, he prayed for the families of men who had been killed and prayed for the POWs he heard being tortured. Praying, Risner says, was as important to most POWs as the tap code. "We gained a lot of strength not only from our private prayers but also from sharing our feelings about God with each other."

To exercise his mind, Risner sometimes said his prayers in Morse code. "I had a piece of rock and the 'Da Da Dits' and the 'Da Da Dit Da's' were echoing around the cell. I said the Twenty-Third Psalm in code and when I finished, Ed Davis in the next cell tapped out in Morse code, 'Say it again.'" The Twenty-Third Psalm, Risner says, "was kind of the prisoner's psalm."

Risner encouraged the development of "study courses, book reviews, entertainment, and language courses, which we held covertly by talking from our separate cells." On Saturday evenings Risner and other POWs would listen to two prisoners talk about movies. "We had two guys who were especially gifted at describing the movies they had seen. Sometimes they would even give us movies that they had never seen but someone else had told them about. . . . We'd lie on our stomachs and listen under the door."

Four days after the Paris Peace Accords were signed on January 23, 1973, North Vietnamese officials assembled 350 POWs to tell them that they were going to be released. Instead of rejoicing, there was silence. The POWs did not want to give the North Vietnamese and the foreign press that were present the satisfaction of seeing them cheer at the news. Instead, Lieutenant Colonel Robbie Risner, the ranking officer, came forward and executed an about-face: "Fourth Allied POW Wing, atten-hut!" he commanded.

The POWs, writes Alfred Townley in *Defiant* (2014), "came to attention, some 350 sandals stamping on the dirt courtyard of Camp Unity, sounding like a small thunderclap. Risner saluted the ranks of POWs facing him. Each squadron commander—the leader of each building or room—snapped a salute in return. Pride shone on the faces of the fighting men assembled in the Hoa Lo Prison. . . . Each of the nine squadron commanders then turned to his men, and together they barked: 'Squadron, dis...missed!'"

In *Faith of My Fathers* (1999) John McCain, who was released a month later, praises Risner's leadership. "From the first moment of his imprisonment to the last, Robbie Risner was an exemplary senior officer, an inveterate communicator, an inspiration to the men he commanded, and a source of considerable annoyance to his captors. Among the longest held prisoners, he suffered the appalling mistreatment regularly inflicted on POWs during the brutal early years of his imprisonment."

McCain called Risner "a genuine American hero." In *When Hell Was in Session* (1997), Jeremiah Denton, a fellow POW, calls Risner "one of the toughest and most honorable men I've ever known who was constantly at work to improve our situation."

Fifteen years after publishing *The Passing of the Night*, Risner wrote an epilogue, in which he mentions that his twenty-nine-year marriage disintegrated and his twenty-six-year-old son Rob died of a congenital heart disorder. "So much has happened, so many dreams unrealized." Nevertheless, there are "so many things to be thankful for."

When Risner died in October 2013, the obituaries praised him as a great fighter pilot and a great leader of men, but there was one negative remark in the *San Antonio Times*. "Over the years, he earned a reputation as a strong leader, one that left him either loved or hated." The obituary writer does not quote anyone who hated Risner, but it is clear that Mary McCarthy hated him.

Risner was one of two airmen McCarthy met on her trip to North Vietnam. She does not name them in *Hanoi,* but when she reissued the book six years later, including it in her collection of essays on Vietnam (*The Seventeenth Degree),* she added a footnote identifying the "older man" as "Robinson ('Robbie') Risner."

McCarthy met the POWs in the living room of a Hanoi villa. She was not sure "whether this was their actual place of confinement." It was not. The North Vietnamese always made sure that visiting delegations interviewed POWs in settings that made it seem as if the POWs were being treated humanely.

McCarthy admits to a certain uneasiness about wanting to meet American POWs. She notes that many anti-war activists who visited North Vietnam did not want to meet them. "Quite a few American visitors shrink from interviewing the pilots . . . [because] it would be painful to meet one's own countrymen in such circumstances." If she knew it would be painful to meet American POWs, why did she meet them?

Moreover, why did she choose to write about the meeting? Susan Sontag also went to North Vietnam and wrote a book about her trip, but she did not write about her meeting with American POWS. Sontag told Frances Kiernan (McCarthy's biographer): "I saw a lot of the things that she [McCarthy] saw and I was taken to see the same prisoners. There we were in this room and there was a guard over to one side. I was really dumb in those days. But I still had my instincts and I thought, This is a terrible situation. I don't understand it and I don't know what's right. So I didn't deal with it in my book."

McCarthy does not say how long the meeting with the two airmen lasted, but she "quickly exhausted" the topics approved by the North Vietnamese: Health, Family, Treatment, Current View of the War. McCarthy first mentions the younger airman, who told McCarthy that "he would have voted for Goldwater if he had been registered in 1964." The younger POW, McCarthy says disdainfully, "seemed wholly unmodified by his experience, and the sole question he put me was 'Can you tell me how the Chicago Cubs are doing?'"

Towards the end of the paragraph McCarthy introduces Risner. "The second prisoner, an older man, had not changed his cultural spots either, except in one respect: he claimed to like Vietnamese candy." McCarthy implies that the two airmen have limited intellects and limited interests. She fails to understand that the two prisoners made innocuous remarks because English-speaking North-Vietnamese officials were present. If the POWS had said anything substantive, they risked being tortured.

McCarthy regards the remarks about the Chicago Cubs and candy as proof positive that the two POWs—indeed all American POWs in North Vietnam—have "low mental attainments." This is what North Vietnamese officials told her. "The Vietnamese . . . have been taken aback by the low mental attainments of the pilots."

McCarthy was dismayed by the POWs' "stiffness of phraseology and naive rote-thinking, childish, like the handwriting on the envelopes the Vietnamese officers emptied from a sack for me to mail." She does not consider the possibility that torture may have affected the POWs' handwriting. The North Vietnamese often wrenched arms out of sockets.

According to McCarthy, the two airmen "had been robotized" by their education and their service in the military. "It had been an insensible process starting in grade school and finished off by the Army." McCarthy quotes North Vietnamese officials to support her negative view of American airmen. The American pilots, one said, were "like beings from a protozoic world." McCarthy admits that she felt "a cultural distance so wide [between herself and the American POWs] that I could see myself reflected in their puzzled, somewhat frightened eyes as a foreigner."

Long before McCarthy visited North Vietnam, she had a negative view of the American military. In 1953 she wrote about a conversation she had with an anti-Semitic Air Force colonel whom she met on a train. McCarthy tries to argue with him, but she comes to the conclusion that he is immune to rational argument. "The desolate truth was that the colonel was extremely stupid." McCarthy implies that the colonel's stupidity is largely the result of his military training.

Being in the American military, McCarthy implies, ruins your mind—especially if you are an officer. Even non-career military men become mentally rigid. In a letter to her friend Hannah Arendt, she says of Charles Bohlen, the Ambassador to Vietnam: "Having been a soldier, he has a kind of natural belligerency that cannot face the idea of a *retreat* from a position."

The essayist Elizabeth Hardwick once said of McCarthy: "I never knew anyone who gave so much pleasure to those around her." McCarthy did not give any pleasure to Risner. Risner's description of the meeting with McCarthy, which appears in *The Passing of the Night*, comes at the end of a chapter entitled "Meeting Foreign Delegations."

The chapter begins: "Of all the indignities we were forced to undergo, I guess I resented meeting the foreign delegations more than any other. . . . There was something so basically inhuman about appearing before delegations and being asked how your food was and having to say it was excellent when it was not. Or to questions of your treatment, to lie in front of cameras and say it was great, when they had literally tortured the stuffing out of you to make you appear."

Risner says he was tortured before and after he met an East German delegation and before and after he met a North Korean delegation, but he does not say he was tortured before he met McCarthy. Perhaps because the North Vietnamese thought he was "doing better," they wanted him to meet "an American—an American woman." North Vietnamese officials warned him: "Do not say anything to disgrace or slander our country. If you do, you will suffer for the rest of the time you are here."

After showing Risner several articles that McCarthy had written, the North Vietnamese made him look presentable and took him to the Plantation, "a nice-looking prison." Several officials were present at the meeting, including the Cat, the name the POWs gave to the North Vietnamese official in charge of torture.

Risner's description of the meeting is brief—comprising only four paragraphs. Risner's third paragraph has a surreal quality. It is about Risner's love of sweets and McCarthy's interest in baking him a cake. "Can I send him a cake?" McCarthy asks. The Cat replies: "He does not need that. We give him plenty of wholesome foods."

In "On Colonel Risner," McCarthy says she does not remember any conversation about a cake. "Although I am a devoted cake-baker, I bake them only for people I like and I did not like Lieutenant Colonel Risner."

In the fourth paragraph Risner says that McCarthy "mentioned hopes for an early end to the war. 'We had better knock on wood,' and she knocked three times on the table . . . [ellipsis Risner's]." McCarthy's knock on wood got Risner in trouble. "I was in interrogation for three hours trying to convince the Dude [a POW name for a North Vietnamese official] that raising eyebrows and knocking on wood were not secret signals."

In the last paragraph Risner expresses his anger at having to meet McCarthy. "I know I suffered because of her request to see me, and to my knowledge she did absolutely nothing to help our cause. This was true of all the appearances." Risner means POW appearances before foreign delegations. The North Vietnamese, Risner notes, only gave visas to anti-war Western journalists.

Early in 1974 Robert Silvers, the editor of the *New York Review of Books*, asked McCarthy to reply to Risner's account of their meeting, and she agreed to do so. In the third paragraph of "On Colonel Risner," McCarthy includes a footnote that she had appended to the new edition of *Hanoi*. Why publish the footnote twice? Perhaps she thought the footnote would have a wider readership if it also appeared in *The New York Review of Books*. Here is the entire footnote.

"This was Robinson ("Robbie") Risner, today a widely admired hardliner and Nixon zealot. From my [original] notes: 'tight lined face, wilted eyes, somewhat squirrely. Fawns on Vietnamese officer. Servile. Zealot. Has seen error of ways. Looks at bananas. Grateful. 'Oh, gee, bananas too?' Speaks of his 'sweet tooth.' Loves the Vietnamese candy. Effusive about it. Perhaps ostracized by his fellow-prisoners. Speaks English slowly, like a Vietnamese practicing the language. Stereotyped language."

Why did McCarthy bring up Risner's politics, which she could only have learned about from Risner's memoir? It is not relevant to what she is discussing, which is an account of their meeting in a North Vietnamese prison. She brought it up to imply that Risner was as untrustworthy as Nixon.

According to McCarthy, Risner was servile because he was afraid of losing the favors the North Vietnamese had granted him. "I guessed that he had been currying favor with his captors and obeyed because of fear that favors would be withdrawn." McCarthy does raise the possibility that Risner was servile because he had been tortured, but "that explanation did not occur to me at the time." Why didn't it occur to her in 1968? Didn't McCarthy know about the television interview with POW Jeremiah Denton in May 1966, when Denton signaled to the world that he had been tortured by blinking the word torture in Morse Code?

Though McCarthy concedes that Risner may have been tortured, she still thinks Risner was untrustworthy. "He was specious in some way I could not have easily defined. . . . I tried to assign his speciousness to this religious streak in him." Risner was a member of the Assembly of God—a Pentecostal Sect. "If I had seen him testifying, with contrite mien, at a revival meeting back in Oklahoma, that probably would have repelled me too."

The main point McCarthy makes in "On Colonel Risner" is that Risner lied about their meeting because he did not want his readers to know that he had been servile. "It is understandable that Risner today does not wish to recall his effusive flattery of his captors, which went far beyond what was called for in the circumstances, but the picture he gives of himself as reluctant, curt, unforthcoming is more than forgetful. It is false."

McCarthy notes that Risner's wife did not respond to a letter she had sent to her, in which she told Mrs. Risner that her husband seemed to be in good health and spirits. In McCarthy's view, Mrs. Risner "did not want to hear about him, having got word through the POW grapevine that in captivity he had become a North Vietnamese toady." McCarthy does not consider the possibility that Mrs. Risner did not want to respond to a writer who welcomed a North Vietnamese victory.

McCarthy's assessment of Risner's character and conduct was wildly off the mark. Risner was not servile. He was one of the most defiant POWs. According to Colonel Gordon Larson, a fellow POW, Risner was "the most influential and effective POW there."

McCarthy wrote "On Colonel Risner" roughly a year after the POWs had been released from North Vietnam. She could have asked Jeremiah Denton or John McCain or hundreds of other former POWs what they thought of Risner, but apparently she did not.

When McCarthy died in 1989, she was praised for her character as well as her writing. Leon Botstein, the President of Bard College, where McCarthy occasionally taught, said McCarthy was "a person of great character." The novelist Mary Gordon observed that McCarthy "combined purity of style with a kind of rigorous moral honesty."

Did the writers who lauded McCarthy's character read what she wrote about Risner?

Why did McCarthy write "On Colonel Risner"? It is not as if her reputation in the academic/literary world had been damaged by what Risner wrote about their meeting. One can reasonably assume that few members of the academic/literary world read Risner's memoir.

McCarthy wrote "On Colonel Risner," I suspect, because she was angered by Risner's effrontery. It is as if she is saying that Risner has some nerve disputing what she said about their meeting. She thinks he is arrogant and vain. "A naive sense of his own importance transpires from the book and this primitive vanity perhaps explains the cake memory: 'a cake just for *him*!'"

"On Colonel Risner" probably was read by very few people, but it did not go unnoticed. In the *Washington Monthly,* James Fallows wrote that McCarthy's essay was "a defensive and quite petty reply to Risner, intended as far as I can tell, to demolish his stature as a witness. . . . Mary McCarthy's hatchet has been bloodied before . . . but the Risner article was the first in which she attacked a defenseless victim."

Anthony Lewis agreed with Fallows. Lewis had also travelled to North Vietnam, and he too had met POWs, but he did not write about his meetings. Lewis does not doubt Risner's veracity. "Risner and others say they were tortured before meeting foreign delegations, to make them promise to say the right things."

"The former prisoners," Lewis notes, "are often critical . . . of American journalists and others who visited Hanoi during the war, saying they were too naive in accepting what they were told about the prisoners and other things. I think the men underestimate the difficulties, and the efforts made to get a sense of the truth, *but there is something to their feelings* [emphasis mine]."

Risner was happy to learn that some anti-war liberals had criticized McCarthy for her portrait of him. He told Frances Kiernan: "Some of her contemporaries, who allegedly were her friends and were liberals like she was, took her to task for what she had done." Risner called McCarthy's depiction of him "character assassination."

Did Risner give much thought to McCarthy's attack? Probably not. In the military world, he was a hero. There is a nine-foot tall statue of him on the grounds of the U.S. Air Force Academy.

McCarthy looked down on Risner and other American POWs, but she greatly admired North Vietnamese military officials. Colonel Ha Van Lau, the head of the North Vietnamese War Crimes Commission, was "a delicate-featured, slender, refined officer, from Hue, of Mandarin ancestry (he reminded me of Prince Andrei in *War and Peace*)."

McCarthy was most impressed by the North Vietnamese leader Pham Van Dong— "a man of magnetic allure, thin, with deep-set brilliant eyes, crisp short electric gray hair." He has courtly manners and he does not employ "the prevailing political cliches."

Though McCarthy grudgingly acknowledges that Risner may have been tortured, she does not think her friend Pham Van Dong knew anything about it. She cannot imagine that this "highly perceptive and intelligent man" would support such a cruel and stupid policy.

Most journalists had a different view of the man who was the head of post-war Vietnam. In July 1979 *New York Times* correspondent Henry Kamm wrote: "Stalin . . . is less unmentionable in Hanoi than in other capitals in the Soviet orbit." Kamm stressed the Stalinist nature of the North Vietnamese regime. "Practitioners of Stalinist policies . . . have shown a marked tendency for carrying out political goals, even when they were economically and socially harmful, with a fanatical perseverance."

Kamm's article focussed on Vietnam's forced expulsion of ethnic Chinese and other people it deemed politically undesirable. Those forced to leave had a choice—either go by boat or go into the jungle. If those being expelled had something the Vietnamese regime coveted—money, gold, jewelry—they were allowed to choose the boat option. "As is the case throughout the rest of the Soviet bloc, the acquisition of convertible currencies, gold or jewels has become one of the principal political objectives of Vietnam."

McCarthy refused to believe that Pham Van Dong was the architect of Vietnam's Stalinist policies. In October 1979 McCarthy told *The Observer,* a British journal: "I've several times contemplated writing a real letter to Pham Van Dong (I get a Christmas card from him every year) asking him can't you stop this, how is it possible for men like you to permit what's going on? One can allow for a certain amount of ignorance at the top for what is executed at a lower level; that's true in any society. But this has gone past that point. I've never written that letter, though; it is still in my pending folder, so to speak. Of course it shouldn't have stayed there, but it did."

In October 1979 McCarthy talked with television interviewer Dick Cavett about post-war Vietnam. Referring to what McCarthy said in *The Observer* about wanting to write a letter to Pham van Dong, Cavett asked her if she had ever written the letter.

McCarthy seemed to be taken aback by the question. She replied that she was planning to write Pham Van Dong, but she wanted to wait until she had more "solid information" about what was happening in Vietnam. Then she sounded more tentative: "I might. I don't know."

Cavett then asked McCarthy: "Why couldn't you call him on the telephone?

"I hate to talk on the phone. A letter is what I ought to write. I still may write the letter."

"Maybe you were wrong about him in the first place?" Cavett asked.

McCarthy seemed flustered by Cavett's question. She became inarticulate. "I don't think one one can be. I've got photos and so on—--and you look at his face and—--anyway. I hope . . . I hope I was not wrong, but he is getting old. It may be that he's no longer directing operations there." McCarthy told Cavett that Pham Van Dong "was the most impressive politician I've ever met . . . . I liked him very very much."

McCarthy ended the discussion by saying to Cavett that she would never send a letter to Pham Van Dong. It would be pointless to do so because Pham Van Dong was old, very old, and therefore powerless "so that the letter could still be written but the real . . . the result might be nil, might be nil, anyway."

According to an obituary in the *New York Times,* Pham Van Dong, who died in 2000, remained a hardline communist. "In retirement, Mr. Dong was a government adviser but he still warned in speeches about the dangers of economic reforms."

Five years after the interview with Cavett, McCarthy speculated that Pham Van Dong probably had lost power as early as 1969, after the death of Ho Chi Minh. Pham Van Dong "was really the carrier of Ho Chi Minh's values and that with the death of Ho Chi Minh, Pham Van Dong became something of a figurehead." This was not the view of other journalists and historians.

In his autobiography, *Out of Step,* Sidney Hook has the following to say about Mary McCarthy. "Although an avowed anti-Stalinist, she traveled to Hanoi and wrote about its Stalinist Communist regime with uncritical enthusiasm, apparently taken in by the blandishments of her hosts, who immediately recognized how vulnerable to their propaganda she had become in virtue of her combination of vanity and guilt. . . . .Mary McCarthy has an almost infinite capacity for self-deception, which enables her to close her eyes to the consequences of words and actions that make her uncomfortable."

Reviewing Frances Kiernan's biography of McCarthy, the critic A.O. Scott quoted McCarthy's remark that the "the writer must be first of all a listener and observer who can pay attention to reality, like an obedient pupil, and who is willing, always, to be surprised by the messages reality is sending through to him." Scott then says: "And so she was, plainly."

To which I would reply: "And so she was not, plainly."

I sent my article to Risner's widow. She replied in a handwritten letter.

Dear Stephen,

Thank you for your essay on Mary McCarthy's encounter with Robbie while he was a POW in Vietnam. Robbie lived life to the fullest and didn't dwell too much on the past. He didn't talk much about it, but I know he felt betrayed by a fellow American as he suffered for her welfare. It does my heart good to read your rebuttal, and even at this late date it makes me realize 'the truth will out.' I only wish Robbie could know that you didn't forget, and that you vindicated him with such a clear, well-written paper. I thank you for him. Steve, I wish you all the best, and appreciate the article more than you will ever know.

God Bless, Dorothy.

This letter was more gratifying than any other words of praise I have ever received for my writing.

CHAPTER 13

Coda, Three Poles: A Poet, a Painter, and a Singer

In *Courier from Warsaw* Jan Nowak writes: "There are crossroads in any man's life that decide his whole future." Twice in my working life I came to a crossroads. In 1973 I chose to leave academia, taking an editorial job with Mathematica; in 1978 I chose to leave the federal government, becoming a Resident Fellow at the American Enterprise Institute. But it is absurd to compare my crosswords with Nowak's. The path I took may have been foolish but it was not dangerous. When Nowak was in the Home Army every path he took was extremely dangerous.

I greatly admire Nowak but I also greatly admire another Polish writer who belonged to the Home Army during World War II: Zbigniew Herbert. He is widely regarded as the greatest Polish poet of the post-war era. My second published essay is entitled "The Poetry of Zbigniew Herbert." I've also read his two works of non-fiction: *Barbarian in the Garden* and *Still Life With A Bridle*.

Herbert was born in Lvov in 1924, which at the time was a Polish city, though now it is in Ukraine. In 1939 it was occupied by the Sovet Union; two years later the Nazis occupied it and they transformed the old city "into a veritable hell," says Charles Simic, a poet/critic. In 1944 Herbert's family moved to Krakow.

Because Herbert had been a member of the Home Army, Poland's post-war Stalinist regime viewed him with suspicion, so he could only get low-paying jobs. He was a primary school teacher, a museum guard, a bank clerk, a shop attendant, a timekeeper in a cooperative, and a librarian. For one year his income came mainly from the money he made from blood donations.

After Stalin died, Herbert got a job as an administrator at the Association of Polish Composers. Moreover, now he could publish his poetry in Poland. In 1958 Herbert got a small grant that enabled him to travel to Western Europe for more than a year. Herbert spent many years living abroad—in Paris, Vienna, Berlin, and Los Angeles. He died in Warsaw in July 1998.

According to the critic Ewa Hryniewicz-Yarborough, when the Polish government granted Herbert a passport they hoped he would never return to Poland. Herbert always returned to Poland, but he rarely stayed very long there. He lived most of his life in Berlin or Paris. Herbert always struggled financially when he was in the West— living mainly on fees from poetry readings, occasional teaching jobs, and money from awards. Simic reports that in 1992 Herbert was "living in great poverty in Paris."

Herbert's non-fiction books are mainly about his travels in Europe and about the art he likes. He praises the paintings in the caves of Lascaux and he praises the great Sienese painters: Duccio, Ambrogio Lorenzetti, and Sassetta. He also writes about the Renaissance painter Piero della Francesca and about the seventeenth- century Dutch painter Gerard ter Borch.

For Herbert the art and literature of Europe—from Lascaux to Matisse—provides solace and sustenance for minds burdened by the horrors of modern history. He says of Piero della Francesca's paintings: "Over the battle of shadows, convulsions, and tumult Piero has erected *lucidus ordo*—an eternal order of light and balance." Great art lives in a timeless present. "Thanks to Sassetta I shall step twice in the same river."

Barbarians in the Garden, which was published in Warsaw in 1962, steers clear of politics, yet there is an oblique criticism of communist regimes. "History . . . teaches that a nation subject to police measures is demoralized, crumbles from within....Even the most ruthless hand to hand combat is less disastrous than whispers, surveillance, fear of one's neighbor, and a scent of betrayal in the air." After his trips to the West Herbert was usually interrogated by the secret police. The police asked him how it was possible for him to leave Poland with five dollars, spend six months abroad, and return with three dollars. His answer was: "I saved." He did not mention that he had been living on awards and grants from Western cultural institutions.

In *Still Life With A Bridle*, which did not appear in Poland until 1993, Herbert praises seventeenth-century Holland, arguing that this bourgeois commercially-oriented society was a place of "freedom, tolerance, and prosperity." He notes that Dutch painters never celebrated military victories. "The Dutch did not leave us a single painting where a defeated adversary is dragged behind a victor's chariot in the dust of spite."

Herbert does not think art can promote political change. "History does not know a single example of art or an artist exerting a direct influence on the world's destiny—and from this sad truth we should be modest, conscious of our limited role and strength." He thinks art that is "engaged"—that directly addresses political questions—is usually banal.

Herbert thinks art should not be self-pitying. "Why the Classics," which was translated by Czeslaw Milosz and Peter Dale Scott, ends with the following lines:

> if art for its subject
> will have a broken jar
> a small broken soul
> with a great self-pity
> what will remain after us
> will be like lovers' weeping
> in a small dirty hotel
> when wallpaper dawns.

The Polish poet Adam Zagajewski says Herbert's poetry possesses "a certain humanist buoyancy, a serenity." Herbert, though, never lets us forget about the darkness of twentieth-century history. (All quotations from Herbert's poetry are from *Zbigniew Herbert, The Collected Poems: 1956-1998.*)

In 1991 Herbert spent some time in Israel after receiving the Jerusalem Prize. There he befriended the Israeli poet Yehuda Amichai. "To Yehuda Amichai," which was translated by Alissa Valles, ends with an oblique allusion to the Holocaust.

> I fall asleep at a fire with my head on my hand
> when night burns out dogs howl and guards go
> to and fro in the mountains.

In Paris Herbert befriended Józef Czapski, a writer and painter who was almost thirty years older than him. Czapski wrote to Herbert: "I love your poems!" In 1958 he painted Herbert's portrait.

Czapski's life is recounted in an elegant biography by Eric Karpeles, *Almost Nothing: The 20th-Century Art and Life of Józef Czapski* (2018). Czapski fought in two wars. He was in the Polish Army in 1917—fighting against the new Soviet state. After being a painter in Paris for more than a decade, Czapski returned to Poland in 1931 and reenlisted in the Polish army in 1939. Captured by the Soviets, he was sent to the Gulag. He and roughly 400 Polish officers escaped the fate of 22,000 Polish officers, including Zbigniew Herbert's uncle, who were murdered by the Soviets in Katyn Forest in April-May of 1940. In the Gulag Czapski lectured on Proust. These lectures were turned into a book: *Lost Time: Lectures on Proust in a Soviet Prison Camp.*

After the Nazis invaded the Soviet Union, Stalin released the Poles in the Gulag and Czapski became an aide to the Polish General Anders, whose army fought for the Allies in Italy. After the war Czapski returned to Paris, where he took up painting again; he also wrote two books about the Soviet Union as well as essays about art.

Reading about Czapski, I was amazed by his ability to think and write and lecture while in prison. After being released, he spent some time in Soviet Central Asia, where he met the poet Anna Akhmatova. Czapski says: "Speaking with me, she said, she breathed a different air, free from the fear that, in Russia, at the time, strangled everyone."

Soldier, writer, painter: Czapski was an extraordinary man. The epigraph to Karpeles' biography of Czapski is from Horace: "If the world should shatter and fall on him,/he would stand fearless among the ruins." (The translation is by Karpeles.)

Nowak, Herbert, Czapski: these Poles stood fearless among the ruins.

Another Pole lifted my spirits—not a writer but a singer: Olga Mieleszczuk. She sings Yiddish tango music—often accompanied by a three-piece band—piano, guitar, and bandoneon—called Tango Attack. I loved her singing and the band's playing, which I discovered by accident on You Tube. I soon found out that her married name was Avigail. She was raised in a devout Catholic Polish family but now she is an Orthodox Jew who lives in Jerusalem. Her husband is an Israeli Jew of Kurdish descent. According to the Jewish Telegraphic Agency, which interviewed her, "Olga Avigail Mieleszczuk's life work is reviving the musical genre of Yiddish tango—two words rarely uttered in the same breath."

Mieleszczuk notes that when she was growing up in Poland she knew nothing about Jews and had never met a Jew. She took an interest in Jewish culture during an interfaith visit to Auschwitz, where she met American and Israeli Jews as well as German grandchildren of Nazi officers. "When I started to sing in Yiddish, I had no idea about Jewish culture at all," she said. Sne enrolled in a course on Yiddish music organized by Warsaw's Shalom Foundation.

"In the 1930s, Warsaw was the capital of the European tango, and most of the songwriters and composers of the tango were Jewish,"

Olga said. But she says that for many Israelis Yiddish belongs to a past that they would rather not think about.

Why do I end this memoir with a brief essay about three Poles? Because they led (and are leading) lives that are inspirational. Reading Herbert, I was struck by his capacity for enjoyment—of art, food, music, walking in a city. Herbert rejects a Stoic withdrawal from the world.

Here is a prose poem by Herbert entitled "Anything Rather Than An Angel" (translated by Czeslaw Milosz and Peter Dale Scott):

If after our death they want to transform us into a tiny withered flame that walks along the paths of winds—we have to rebel. What good is an eternal leisure on the bosom of air, in the shade of a yellow halo, amid the murmur of two-dimensional choirs?

One should enter rock, wood, water, the cracks of a gate. Better to be the creaking of a floor than shrilly transparent perfection.